BRIDGET ASHTON

Hit the Road, Gals

ASTONISHING HITCHHIKING ADVENTURES
IN THE 1960S

The Book Guild Ltd

First published in Great Britain in 2024 by
The Book Guild Ltd
Unit E2 Airfield Business Park,
Harrison Road, Market Harborough,
Leicestershire. LE16 7UL
Tel: 0116 2792299
www.bookguild.co.uk
Email: info@bookguild.co.uk
Twitter: @bookguild

Copyright © 2024 Bridget Ashton

All photos by the author, except for one

The right of Bridget Ashton to be identified as the author of this work has been asserted by them in accordance with the Copyright, Design and Patents Act 1988.

All rights reserved. No part of this publication may be reproduced, transmitted, or stored in a retrieval system, in any form or by any means, without permission in writing from the publisher, nor be otherwise circulated in any form of binding or cover other than that in which it is published and without a similar condition being imposed on the subsequent purchaser.

The events in this book all took place over half a century ago. They all really happened, but some perhaps slightly differently owing to the tricks of memory. In only one case has a name has been changed to protect an identity

Typeset in 11pt Minion Pro

Printed and bound in the UK by TJ Books LTD, Padstow, Cornwall

ISBN 978 1916668 157

British Library Cataloguing in Publication Data.
A catalogue record for this book is available from the British Library.

*To Jenny, Mary, Tonie and Chris
and all the other adventurous gals of the 1960s*

'In the 1960s, when young women are expected to settle down and marry, Bridget and her friends from Hereford College of Education dream of bigger landscapes - partly inspired by the *Mappa Mundi* in the city's cathedral and their sixpenny road maps. The reader hitchhikes with the trainee teachers through the UK and Ireland, France, Italy, Spain and North Africa. Her use of diary extracts and photos ensures that we share the danger, romance and onion sandwiches.'

Barbara Fox, author of
Is the Vicar in, Pet? and *Bedpans and Bobby Socks*

'The further back Bridget Ashton delves into her immature apprenticeship as a latter-day Freya Stark or Egeria, the sharper her pen; the more ironic, funny and daring her writing becomes. With Hit the Road, Gals, she hits her stride, as if there is not a moment to be lost on life's wondrous yellow brick road.'

Max Adams, author of
Unquiet Women and *The Wisdom of Trees*

'In 1963 Bridget steps out of her teacher training college door and straight onto the road to adventure, armed only with a cheap map, stout stick, and enormous zest for life. It's fascinating to come with her on the journey.'

Biddy Carrdus, cultural historian

'These immature girls threw themselves cheerfully into X-rated dangers, despite the efforts of the principal of their all-female college to restrain them. Hitchhiking along the roads of the 1960s, often so hungry that they stole scraps of bread and yet singing as they went, they confronted so many perils that you hold your breath.'

Ian Leech, editor of
Inside Morpeth magazine

By the Same Author

Cold War, Warm Hearts, 2023
Hay Before the Bookshops or The Beeman's Family, 2022

Bridget Gubbins' Morpeth Local History series
De Merlay Dynasty, 2018
The Conquest of Morpeth, 2017
Juliana and Ranulph of Morpeth Castle, 2016
Newminster: Monks, Shepherds and Charters, 2014
The Mysteries of Morpeth's Workhouse, 2013
The Drovers are Coming to Morpeth Town, 2012
The Curious Yards and Alleyways of Morpeth, 2011

Power at Bay, 1997
Generating Pressure, 1991

Contents

Introduction	xi
Maps	xiv
Prologue	xvi

1. She Really Gave You Permission?
   HEREFORD, AUTUMN 1963 — 1

2. Singing Garçons
   FRANCE, EASTER 1964 — 13

3. Grasshoppers And Bullfights
   SPAIN, FRANCE, SUMMER 1964 — 26

4. Roads In The North
   HEREFORD, AUTUMN 1964 — 54

5. Unknown Land
   IRELAND, HEREFORD, SUMMER 1965 — 65

6. Long Hot Roads South
   FRANCE, ITALY, SICILY, SUMMER 1965 — 81

7. Call Of The Desert
      NORTH AFRICA, SPAIN, SUMMER 1965   106

8. This Land Is Our Land
      ENGLAND, SCOTLAND, WALES, IRELAND, AUTUMN 1965   152

9. Holy Week
      SPAIN, EASTER 1966   203

10. Towards The Peak
      WALES, IRELAND, HEREFORD, SUMMER 1966   226

11. Scattering
      HEREFORD, JULY 1966   247

12. Epilogue   249

Further Reading   251
Acknowledgements   255
About the Author   256

Introduction

Between 1963 and 1966, I was one of the three hundred girls at an all-female teacher training college in Hereford. Poised on the threshold of adulthood, we were no longer dependent girls nor yet mature women, not quite one thing nor yet the other. Aged mainly between eighteen and twenty-two years of age, our lives stretched ahead of us, tantalising, sometimes frightening, full of every possibility.

Our naivety must seem astonishing to present-day young women, who have often travelled widely and have access to the internet and instant communication with their friends through their mobile phones. We wrote letters and waited days for replies. We dropped pennies into public phone boxes with a big clunk, and talked until the money ran out. We knew only British food. A long French loaf of bread was a great surprise, and a pizza almost unheard of. Travelling around was by train or bus, on roads far less cluttered with traffic than now. Hitchhiking opened up the world to people on limited budgets. This was the era of Jack Kerouac's *On the Road*.

These stories from fifty years ago are all true. The earlier ones rely largely on memory, holiday scrapbooks and photographs of poor quality. About halfway through the three-year college course

I started a daily diary that allowed me to summarise and date the episodes more precisely. I didn't know at the time that I'd write a book fifty years later, and I now find much of the writing naive, even embarrassing. When including diary excerpts, I often felt the urge to recreate them in more mature language, but I generally resisted the temptation. Authenticity triumphed over literacy. It tells more truly how we young women of the 1960s experienced our world.

Spring 2024

Introduction

College of Education, Hereford, 1964. Photo with kind permission of Herefordshire History.

The Songs

As we moved along the roads, we sang. We learned new songs wherever we could, from different cultures and languages, and we thought we might use them as future teachers. We heard pop songs on the radio; some of us had record players; and we went to folk clubs.

Many of the songs are mentioned in the text, but the quotations cannot be included in the text for fear of infringing copyright.

It is always possible for curious readers to investigate for themselves the songs that influenced us. And then to picture us, hair blowing in the wind, as we made our way along the roads, or tentatively plucking our guitars in folk clubs, or joining in the Irish festivals. Our world in the 1960s was one of the Beatles and the Rolling Stones, of Bob Dylan and Joan Baez, the Irish Rovers and the Dubliners. Our joyful enthusiasm for life was expressed in song. Wherever went, we sang.

The author, 2024

Prologue

I WILL MARRY YOU, MADAME
ATLAS MOUNTAINS, 17 AUGUST 1965

"Are you going to Marrakesh?" Mary asks the driver.
It is afternoon in the Moroccan desert town of Zagora.
"*Oui, oui, Marrakesh.*" The lorry driver nods. We agree a time to meet him in the evening. When we arrive, he indicates that we must clamber onto the open back of the lorry. We scramble up, pulling our baskets behind us onto crates of empty bottles. Here we must make ourselves comfortable.

We settle down for a long ride north across the High Atlas Mountains. We leave the Sahara behind, the lorry bumping and shaking us and the bottles rattling noisily in their crates.

Every so often, the lorry stops and a man in loose flowing robes climbs up or another one leaves. There is room in the cab for one or two besides the driver, but from time to time a man joins us on the crates. This one grins at us cheerfully, pointing and constantly saying, "*Bonjour, M'sieu.*" As many times as we say, "*Bonjour, M'selle*," pointing to ourselves, he simply repeats "*Bonjour, M'sieu*" and chuckles some more. We are a tired, rattling little group on the crates of bottles. After a long uphill climb, the lorry pulls over to cool the engine on the roadside. An enormous cliff falls precipitously down to our right in the black depths of the stony mountainside.

Suddenly, "Happy birthday to you…" Mary sings forth in the silence of the night.

What is this? I realise that midnight has passed, and the date is 17 August 1965. It is the morning of my twenty-first birthday.

She pulls a birthday cake out of her basket. It is a packet of biscuits and a thick household wax candle. Next comes a parcel containing pomegranates she has raided from an orchard and a sprig of unripe dates. She hands me a card she has created showing a camel made from Sahara sand.

"*Merci*, Marie," I say, and give her a hug in the darkness.

We invite the driver and the young boy with him in the cab to our party. M'sieu Man goes off to take a turn sleeping in the cabin, while the four of us light the candle and share out the biscuits.

The driver has decided that we should rest here for some hours. We manage to snuggle down on the crates of bottles, using our clothes and baskets for pillows, and somehow drift into an uneasy sleep. When the driver makes an improper move, I wake up and get rid of him by swearing at him so fiercely in English that he backs off. After an interval a young man climbs up onto the back of the lorry. My diary:

> *Handshakes, beams, friendship all round, and off the pair of them went down among the scanty bushes of the mountain side. I guess if woman won't be man's best friend, man will make do with man!*
>
> *We woke as the sun rose and began the drive through the last of the jagged Atlas mountains. It was cold, and rained a little, pattering on our faces as we rolled along the stony desert road.*

Mary and I move into the shelter of the cab. I am seated next to the driver, who continues to show an unsuitable interest in me.

I gradually learn my value in Morocco. He offers me many *mille francs*. As I determinedly keep on looking out of the window, saying, "*Non, non, M'sieu,*" he keeps putting up the price, which I translate mentally into pounds. When he gets as high as £5, he realises I can't be bought. Both his French and mine are limited, but I understand the following well enough. "*Madame, je vous épouserai!*" Madame, I will marry you!

***

The story of my twenty-first birthday and the marriage proposal on the back of the lorry in the Atlas Mountains begins in a town in the west of England.

1

She Really Gave You Permission?

HEREFORD, AUTUMN 1963

It started with our mothers in 1963. I am holding up a small piece of paper. It has caused my friends to cluster round me and is addressed to the principal of our strict all-girls college in Hereford. I read it out:

> Dear Miss Hipwell,
> I am not forbidding my daughter Bridget to hitchhike. She is of the age to make her own decisions and must be free to use her own judgement. I relieve you of responsibility.
> Yours sincerely
> Eileen M Ashton.

"Did she really write that?" says Mary. "My mother would never give permission."

"Nor mine," says Tonie. "She would faint if she knew what we did."

"I wouldn't even dare ask my mother," says Jenny. "It would only give her ideas."

Gangling, leggy girls we are, wild and inscrutable, clustered together at Hereford College of Education. We are being trained to be schoolteachers and at the same time we are learning about hitchhiking. The roads out of town are leading us into adventures, towards uncertain destinies, routes to life and love.

But Miss Hipwell is discovering what we are up to. She had called us in, speaking sternly. "You must understand that I cannot permit this behaviour. The college is acting *in loco parentis*. That means that, while you are here, we are acting in the place of your parents. Hitchhiking is dangerous. You don't know who is driving the vehicle. Bad things can happen."

We had demurred. We are eighteen and nineteen years of age. "But my mother knows I do it," I say.

"I find it unlikely that your parents would agree if they knew exactly what you do," she had said. She is prim, in her early forties, with short, tight hair. "If they knew that you stay out late, disobey the rule to sign in by 10.30, which is devised for your safety, any responsible parent would forbid this behaviour."

We had left her feeling rueful and resentful. Consequently I had written to my mother asking for help, and she replies with the note removing responsibility from the college. I hear nothing more on the subject from Miss Hipwell. My friends will probably quietly ignore the ruling. If we are back by the 10.30 pm curfew, our movements are not easily traceable.

***

It Is Sweet And Fair To Walk For The Country

Hereford, autumn 1963

At my interview, Miss Bookham said to me, "We don't have any Welsh-language classes here. But, as you have made Hereford your first choice of college, I'll take a chance with you, Miss Ashton."

I am one of the 1963 intake of a hundred girls, adding to the two hundred already here. We are a rather ordinary set of young women, not the kind you would expect to read about in great dramas or romantic novels. Our parents are tradesmen, lower-level civil servants, housewives, shop assistants or secretaries, that sort of thing, and my father is the county beekeeping adviser in Northumberland.

The college takes its role to protect our virtue seriously, and our families expect us to make respectable marriages. Schoolfriends who left school before us, and are working in shops or factories, often display their engagement rings. Like them, we also want to meet the men of our dreams, but we certainly know from Bob Dylan's song that the times they are a-changin'.

At the centre of the city of Hereford is another world, that of the cathedral's *Mappa Mundi*. This map is six and a half centuries old. Hanging in a shady aisle, its great vellum circle over four feet in diameter is set in a wooden, pentagonal frame shaped like the gable of a house. It illustrates every significant place in the world as it was then known, and God's plan for humanity, their life after death in heaven or hell. Jerusalem, the most important city in Christendom, is placed at the centre of the map. Asia occupies the top half, and Europe and Africa take a lower quarter each. Hereford can be seen faintly in the west, near Gloucester, Worcester, Shrewsbury and the prominent nearby Clee Hill. The River Wye may be faintly discerned.

But we have our sixpenny Esso road maps. Nothing could be more different from the *Mappa Mundi*. From our centre at Hereford, the maps show red lines of roads radiating outward in all directions. The A49 heads north towards Scotland, or south towards Ross-on-Wye. From there, connections lead off towards Bristol or London. The A4103 runs towards Worcester and on to Birmingham. The A438 leads into Wales, towards Hay-on-Wye and Brecon, and thence to Carmarthen and Pembroke Dock. The A465 heads south-westerly towards Abergavenny and on to Cardiff.

From my room in the student hostel, on the distant horizon I can see the Black Mountains. When I look beyond the pines on the lawn and the rooftops of the suburban street towards the setting sun, there are the hills of Wales. Many of us have close connections. Val comes from Denbigh in the north, Tonie is from Pembrokeshire, Bethan, a Welsh language speaker, is from Llanelli, and my childhood home is the border town of Hay-on-Wye. As Miss Hipwell has found, we are learning to travel along these roads, walking, breathing in the air from the hills, hitching rides, absorbing the landscape as our own. We too are becoming pilgrims, walkers, explorers, crossing our known world. To walk is to learn to care about the land. Tonie, who knows some Latin, has a motto: *Dulce et decorum est pro patria ambulare.* It is sweet and fair to walk for the country.

Songs And Hills

We may decide to go up and away in a single instant. Tonie and I have spent a morning singing. We are both geography students, and we decide we will go to Wales for the afternoon with her guitar and my mouth organ to seek out Welsh songs and to learn about the landscape. Taking our sixpenny road map, we leave Hereford following the A49 road signs north, and heading for Montgomery.

As we walk along, we raise our thumbs and smile in the faces of the approaching drivers. It is important to look encouraging.

"I can take you to Craven Arms. You can go from there towards Montgomery," says the friendly man who stops with his van. We always need to assess the driver because we will be stepping into a moving vehicle that we can't control. But this man seems to be a safe bet. He signals for us to climb onto the back of his van, and the wind blows our hair into knots as we head northward.

Two handsome young men give us our next lift. We pass through pleasant green countryside, following a winding river through the hills. Longmynd, the Long Mountain, a great mass of ancient pre-Cambrian rock, lies to our north. I fall instantly in love with one of the men. This is the problem. We are constantly exposed to temptation. What do we do if we fall for a gorgeous man whom we will surely meet in our travels? In this case, the men drop us off with a nonchalant and friendly "Cheerio". My love must be left unrequited. By mid-afternoon we have crossed the border into Wales.

The town of Montgomery has a big castle on a cliff. We find it a quiet, ghost-like place, with closed shops and Welsh people withdrawing into their houses. We feel a resistance to strangers and a shut-out feeling. The English border is only three miles to the east, and the castle was built by the invading Norman lord Roger Montgomery. The Welsh were threatened by the foreigners, by intruders, people who don't belong there, like us.

We walk on towards Welshpool. Blue rainclouds are descending and, not having umbrellas, we pick great butterbur leaves on long stalks and hold them over our heads, thinking ourselves very enterprising. At last, we come to a tiny canal with an old bridge over it. The canal is blocked and full of brown stagnant water and zipping flies. It smells of sweet elder and sour nettle. The water is covered with golden water lilies.

Under a leaf in the water is a tiny cocoon of a caterpillar, sealed and glued. It has cut a small bit out of the big lily leaf and stuck itself there between the layers. It is fat and wriggly, with an orange speckled face.

We haven't learned any new Welsh songs yet, so we continue towards Welshpool. By now it is early evening, Saturday night in a small Welsh town reminding me of Hay-on-Wye. Young people are strolling around, a juke box is sounding from the open door of a café, pub doors are opening and closing, lights turning on in the houses, all in the calm, warm wet air.

We admire the black and white half-timbered inn on the main street, but we can't stop. We need to get back to Hereford before

10.30 pm or we will be locked out of our student accommodation. Our first lift homeward takes us to Shrewsbury, and then we head south on the A49 towards Hereford, where we find ourselves on a quiet stretch of road.

Tonie is feeling glum. We've seen new towns and pretty landscapes, but when you are in love and separated from your man you are restless and discontented.

"We'll send Ivor a message," she says. She knows that Ivor will be driving his lorry down this road tomorrow. We seek out some light-coloured stones with which we can scratch words on the dark asphalt road surface. Traffic is only intermittent and there is nothing to stop us. On the left lane of the two-lane highway, we draw in great big capital letters:

IVOR
HIYA
IVOR

We feel sure he will see our message as he drives south the next day.

Back in good time, we establish ourselves on the lawn outside our student hostel, which overlooks the great redbrick Gothic building of our college. Tonie has her guitar. We orchestrate our three-chord version of "Myfanwy" to our own satisfaction, if not to any great musical standard.

The hills of Wales on the distant western horizon are softly fading from our view while we sing the beautiful Welsh love song.

The roads west continue to tempt us. There are coracle fishermen in Wales, and we can go to find them. My friend Chris and I walk out of Hereford, pass near Hay-on-Wye and join the A40 to Carmarthen. We are aiming for the Teifi river and there we are successful. The fisherman's little round boat is made of a framework of woven willow rods covered by a tarred outer canvas layer and has a simple board seat just about big enough for two people. He is smartly dressed in a flat cap, shirt, collar and tie, and lets us have a ride in his boat with him, one at a time. Steering with one oar, his other hand is free for his fishing rod. This is the best kind of geography lesson.

As we develop our hitchhiking skills, the world opens up to us with the help of our Youth Hostel Association handbook. It shows where the hostels are to be found all over England and Wales, in both wild countryside and city centres. If we fancy a weekend break away from college, we can go to Staunton on Wye, a village half a dozen miles from Hereford that has a youth hostel in a massive Gothic building. The overnight charge is three shillings. We make friends with the warden and sleep in bunk beds in freezing cold dormitories, under heavy damp grey wool blankets. By cooking our own food, often smuggled from the college kitchen, we keep the cost down to nearly nothing. Bread and Spanish onion sandwiches for breakfast is one of our specialities. We know the rules – doors locked at 10.30 pm, a job given to us every morning such as sweeping the stairs or cleaning the kitchen, no alcohol, and separate dormitories for males and females.

Miss Hipwell may wish we didn't do this sort of thing, but the momentum is unstoppable.

FIFTY MILES
STRATFORD-UPON-AVON, 7–8 FEBRUARY 1964

Sometimes, the older method of getting from one place to another takes priority. We walk.

"I just can't wait for tomorrow," Chris says to me one Friday afternoon. We have tickets for a college-organised coach visit to the Royal Shakespeare Theatre in Stratford-upon-Avon for the Royal Ballet's performance of Tchaikovsky's *Sleeping Beauty* the next night. I love the music and have never seen the live performance.

"We could leave now," I say. "Why don't we walk?" We resolve to do this without hitchhiking. It is about fifty miles if we go direct. We pack a few essentials in our ex-army khaki haversacks, and, supported by our sturdy sticks, off we go. We must arrive in time for the performance at 7.30 pm on Saturday, the next day.

Nothing daunts us. Wearing our fashionable duffle coats and green and silver college scarves, we take the main road out of Hereford towards Bromyard and Worcester. We are walking well. The traffic does not deter us and gets less frequent as the hours go by. By midnight we arrive at Worcester, a distance of about twenty-five miles. Certainly we are tiring, but mainly we need the public conveniences. When we find them, a woman rushes out past us.

She is pulling a bag behind her. We are shocked. This kind of on-the-road lifestyle is not attractive. The toilet block must be where she is spending the night.

On we go, using our road map to show us the most direct way. We've eaten our stores of food, and by two in the morning we realise we must get some rest. Looking out for shelter, we find an open barn full of hay bales. Clambering up, we collapse into dead sleep. A few hours later, we wake frozen and stiff.

Now our problems really start because our legs have tightened up. We can only walk slowly and stumblingly and we have another twenty-five miles to go. As we struggle on, one step after another, we obstinately refuse to try to get a lift. We pass a little café in a village and drink some tea to warm us up. At midday we find a chip shop. The trouble is that we can no longer bend our legs. This is not too difficult when we are on a flat strip of road, but when there is a downward slope it is necessary to make little jumps, one leg after another, because our legs won't bend. By the time we are three miles from Stratford, we really cannot move at all, and dump ourselves down on the roadside.

We'll have to give in. It is really mortifying to be so close but not able to complete the distance. We scramble into an upright position, and hold up our thumbs at the approaching cars. Soon we have a lift to Stratford and head for the address of my mother's cousin Rita. We had an arrangement in advance to visit her before the performance. She is my godmother, and I haven't seen her since I was a child, and too young to remember. Likewise, she doesn't know what to expect of me.

We ring the bell. She stands and looks in amazement. We are speechless, leaning on our sticks, so exhausted we can hardly say a word. "You'd better come in and get warm," she says kindly. She gives us hot drinks while she runs a bath. When it is my turn, I immediately fall asleep in the warmth of the water.

Chris and I are determined to see *Sleeping Beauty*. Fed amply by Cousin Rita, and now thawed out a little, we stumble the short distance to the theatre.

"Up the stairs on the right," says the attendant checking our tickets. Our college has booked the cheapest tickets in the highest level. Four flights of stairs await us. Pressing against the wall, moving our legs into bendy positions and leaning on our long sticks, we struggle upwards one step at a time.

Two zombie-like creatures join their fellow students, already seated. The music begins. It is wonderful, probably, but we both fall sound asleep so we don't know. When it is time for the lovely waltz, one of my favourite pieces of music, I shake myself into life. I hold open the eyelids of both my eyes between my fingers and thumbs, but it is no use. We are dead to the world, two real-life sleeping beauties.

Rules
Hereford, March 1964

"Mary, please will you sign us in?" Tonie and Val are out on the road somewhere near Abergavenny.

They had taken their guitars and sat playing them on a roundabout, puzzling and at the same time entertaining the drivers of the lorries and cars that passed by. "This Land Is Your Land" they had been singing, and they meant the land of Wales rather than the USA of Woody Guthrie. They will not be back before the 10.30 curfew, and so they are ringing the single telephone in the student hostel. One of the passing students answers it and summons Mary from her room.

Waiting for a suitable moment when no-one is looking, Mary forges their names in the signing-in book and goes to bed.

Around midnight, there is a knock on her door. Miss Aiken, the grey-haired tutor in charge of the hostel, is standing there in her blue dressing gown and slippers. "Miss Barrow, do you know where Miss Jones and Miss Bonnell are tonight? Did you sign them in?"

What could she say? She is summoned to Miss Hipwell next day for a reprimand. Tonie and Val are roundly chastised too. The rule is immutable. We must be signed in by 10.30. Our girlish reputations must be safeguarded.

I NEED AN ATLAS
HAY-ON-WYE, MARCH 1964

Our student grants must be stretched out as far as possible, and one thing I don't want to spend money on is books. There are two essential volumes that geography students must buy, cheap paperback versions of mildly academic tomes: Dudley Stamp's *Britain's Structure and Scenery* and A E Trueman's *Geology and Scenery in England and Wales*. They cost five shillings each. Other books that we are supposed to buy I borrow from libraries. There are too many important things to spend money on rather than books, such as going to the jazz or folk music clubs, where one must buy at least one drink. However, there is one book I simply must have, and a new one would be expensive. I decide to go to Hay-on-Wye.

"Would you like to show me your atlases?" I ask the young woman assistant. I am at the new second-hand bookshop in Hay in the former fire station. It has been opened by Richard Booth, the man who has just purchased Hay Castle. I choose a big atlas with a hard red cover that costs me only two pounds. Leaving the shop, I walk along Castle Street towards the square overlooked by Hay's castle, and then to 3 Market Street, where I used to live as a child. Hay is an old-fashioned market town of no special status. I make my way to the bridge over the Wye and up the Clyro road towards Hereford. My new atlas is my treasure. I'll use it to plan future expeditions.

2

Singing Garçons

France, Easter 1964

"We don't speak French!" Jenny protests. We are sitting at the table of the college dining hall. Jenny pushes her long brown wavy hair aside. She can always see the problems.

Spreading thick New Zealand butter across the slice of bread on her plate, Mary disputes this. "It is true, but we can manage. We can use hand signals. And learn some French before we go: bread, jam, cheese, words for all the things to eat." She spreads the bright-red raspberry jam on her bread and butter.

"French boys – I wonder what they are like," ponders Tonie. She deeply loves her native Wales and cannot imagine falling in love with anyone beyond it.

We consider how we could get to France. It would mean hitchhiking as far as Dover to catch the boat to France. Mary is the only one of us to have gone abroad. She had been on a school trip to Switzerland when she was thirteen years old. Her strongest memory of that visit is the cherry jam she had spread on her crispy breakfast rolls in the morning. Going to France on our own is quite a different matter.

"Perhaps it will be dangerous?" suggests Lindy, refusing a jam doughnut. She wants to keep her trim figure. "French men may threaten you. How will you protect yourself?"

"You could use pepper," says Val. "You shake it all over them and they sneeze so much that you can run away!" We'll need to think about that. But we also have the idea that French boys are charming, good-looking, Gallic and romantic.

The idea of crossing the sea is in our minds every day as we get gradually plumper from the liberally supplied bread, butter and jam for our afternoon tea.

Mary needs some funds. Her grant has run out, and her father is unlikely to help her. She has an appointment at the Midland Bank in Hereford city centre and climbs the stone steps of the building on the corner of Widemarsh Street. A little while later she comes out, feeling abashed. She follows the street past the cattle market and the boys' school on her left. She passes the Essex pub on her right and the big hotel on the left where the jazz club is held on Wednesday nights, both places which attract us and our limited funds. Up and over the railway bridge she goes, the brick tower of the college appearing through the trees on the hill. She drops herself onto the bed in Tonie's room. "Well, what did he say?" we all ask her in a rush.

"He refused," she says. "He was kind, but he told me that if I needed money I could go potato picking." This is what country women do to earn some spending money. But it is an unlikely suggestion for Mary. If we want to go to France, we'll have to manage with the little money we have.

The three-week Easter vacation approaches, and out of the half-dozen of us who had originally sat at that table only Mary and I remain determined. She is strong, willing, ready to have a go at anything including encountering bank managers and like me she is from a rural background. We have ten pounds between us and have rummaged up the extra two pounds each way for the boat fare. As geography students, we want to learn all we can about the world, the land, the farms, and naturally the French *garçons* too.

Randomly consulting our atlases, we decide to head for the Massif Central, a mountainous landscape formed by ancient volcanos.

***

Fish Soup And Songs
Clermont-Ferrand, 25–29 March 1964

Pierre and Jean Luc are in the kitchen of the *auberge de jeunesse*, the youth hostel, in Clermont-Ferrand. They appear with a pot of soup that they place on the table. Two sleek young men, with neatly trimmed black beards and short dark hair, have made our acquaintance.

"*Potage de poisson!*" Fish soup. We share our bread and cheese, and Mary enjoys the soup. I explain that I am vegetarian. We tell them our names, *Marie* and *Brigitte*. "*Brigitte Bardot!*" they respond, laughing at my name, which is the same as that of the seductive film star. We manage to chatter happily enough in our own languages, they having no English and we virtually no French. We smile and say please and thank you, and agree next day to make a trip into the mountains with them in their car.

Finally, after three days, we have arrived where we want to be. We had crossed over on the ferry from Dover to Calais and, fortified with a long stick each, a jar of pepper to scare away potential assaulters in our pockets and rucksacks on our backs, we'd walked away from the boat in the grey dawn of the March morning. Our first experience of French young men had been dozens of them approaching us from behind on mopeds, toot-toot-tooting and causing us to jump back in fright. Instead of a pavement, we'd found that we were walking in a special lane for scooters.

We had made good progress hitchhiking south from Calais. "*Vous allez où, M'sieu?*" we had practised saying. Where are you going, sir? Lifts are easy, and we have a French road map.

Crossing the rolling plains of Picardy, we'd noticed the ploughed and cultivated strips of farmland. There were no hedgerows as in England and Wales, and the strips reminded us of the three-field rotation of medieval England that we'd learned about in school. In Paris we'd rattled in the wooden underground trains to Laumière youth hostel, where we found an international company of young people, Germans, French, Dutch and North Africans. Paris is illustrated on Hereford Cathedral's *Mappa Mundi* as an important city, and it is the same for us as twentieth-century pilgrims. We are fascinated to meet people who speak so many different languages, and the North Africans who write our names for us in their exotic flowing Arabic script. But we can't linger. Paris is an expensive city to be passed through as quickly as possible, and we are country girls.

Next day, we make our way south along the *Route Nationale 7* using the same trick we'd learned in London: take the Metro to the last stop along the line in the direction of travel. Hitching is straightforward, but lifts in three-lane road are terrifying. Vehicles overtaking from opposite directions compete for the centre lane, and we gasp in fear at several narrow escapes. Nevertheless, we arrive unharmed in Clermont-Ferrand, where we meet Jean Luc

and Pierre and are being exposed for the first time to fish soup.

The following day, we accept their invitation to visit the mountains. We squeeze ourselves in the back of Jean Luc's little car. He is driving, and Pierre is with him in the front.

"*Allons enfants de la Bourgogne*", the boys begin to sing as we drive up the winding roads into the hills. What is this? Boys, singing, in harmony, for sheer joy? This is surprising. It is not something we'd ever experience in England. Over the next few hours and the following day too, we learn more French songs. Our favourite is one about the king of Spain, who dances with the black-eyed girls all night on the mountain.

The chorus contains words that sound like "*digga digga dong*". We can only guess what they mean. The song may be part of a seduction routine, but meanwhile the romance is enchanting.

The boys stop the car at a café near a tumbledown castle. There are no notices to say what it is. It seems to be half abandoned, just lying there with weeds and scrubby bushes growing over it. We follow the boys into the bar and seat ourselves round a table.

"*Alors! Mangeons!*" Let's eat. Pierre empties the contents of a bag onto the table. Bread, sausage, cheese and butter tumble out. The delicious long *pain* of France is cut up and made into sandwiches. The owner of the bar is clearly used to his customers bringing their own food. The boys buy red wine for all of us. This is what we'd come to France for, delicious food, singing French boys, and wine in a village bar. *Très bien!*

Off we go towards the village of Champeix. No-one seems to think about connecting wine and the dangers of driving. I spot some poultry pecking around beside the road, and I decide I'll teach Mary some French. After all, I have the advantage of two years' French tuition at school when I was eleven and twelve, and Mary has none at all. It takes a while, but in the end she announces to Jean Luc and Pierre in the front: "*Le coq et la poule sont sur la route.*" The cock and the hen are on the road. We giggle as the boys look around. Indeed, the fowls had been on the road, quite a few kilometres back.

We get out to walk a little, and then we see approaching us a sight out of a story book. A man is leading two oxen yoked to a cart loaded high with wood, his dog at his heels. He pulls up to chat, and he and the boys exchange polite compliments.

"Bridget, he's wearing wooden clogs," Mary says. Realising this is something very unusual for English girls, the boys joke with him, and he merrily does a little dance for us, clippety cloppety. *Sabots*. We learn the French word for clogs. To add to our education in music and French culture, the boys teach us a song in the car on the way back, "*En passant par la Lorraine avec mes sabots*". Its *one-and-two-and / one-and-two-and* rhythm gets us singing merrily in French.

They take us back safely to the youth hostel in Clermont-Ferrand. Soon we must go our separate ways, they to Metz in eastern France, where they live, and us into the mountains of the Massif Central. They invite us to visit them in Metz, where we can stay in a youth hostel in a nearby forest. We agree to do this on our return route to England. We'll be safe. All youth hostels have separate dormitories for boys and girls, and a warden to keep an eye on things.

Mountain Landscape
Chambon, 30 March–2 April 1964

We get lifts into the mountains as far as the village of Chambon-sur-le-Lac in the Vallée de Chaudefour. There is a youth hostel here, a two-storey partially converted stone farmhouse. The wardens, with the friendly French titles of *Père* and *Mère Aubergiste*, are homely country people. We are shown our dormitory on the first floor. Like all youth hostels, there are bunk beds in iron frames with coarse grey woollen blankets, and we bring our own cotton sheet sleeping bags. We may cook our food in the hostel kitchen.

The Vallée de Chaudefour is wide and open, surrounded by steep mountains. The peaks at the upper end are still snow-covered in this early spring weather, and streams lead down to the nearby Lac Chambon. We can study geography here. But first, most importantly, we must find our food. Early next morning, we walk to Chambon village and the first stop is the *boulangerie*, the bakery. The bread we are familiar with in England is usually sliced and wrapped in waxed paper, nothing like the long newly baked French *pain* that we find here. We buy peach jam, which we have never had before. With our supplies, we wander down towards the lake.

"*Bonjour, M'selles.*" A friendly young man greets us at the lakeside. He introduces himself as Danny, and he is with his friend Serge. We share our picnic in the sunshine. Danny tells us he is a butcher boy in the nearby town of Murol.

We agree to go out with them in the evening and they collect us at the hostel in Danny's car. In a little Murol bar, we dance to the French pop singer Johnny Hallyday. When it is time to leave, Serge takes Mary in his car, and I go with Danny. We've had a little wine, and we are cheerful. But I am not as cheerful as he thinks, and protest strongly when my seat, next to the driver's, suddenly slides back into a horizontal position. Is this how French boys court their girlfriends? It's not for me. He grins good-naturedly and drives me back.

Over the next few days, we explore the landscape. Although this area is a valley shaped by glaciers from ancient times, there are also igneous rocks formed by volcanic activity. We find a cave with an overhanging cliff of hexagonal basalt columns, and eroded exposures of granite stones among which are examples of "onion weathering". These rounded rocks are made of layers of stone that can be peeled away, inside which amethysts may occasionally be found. Also, we look at the moraines, mounds of earth dumped by the melting glaciers blocking the river and forming Lac Chambon. We discover *roches moutonées*, sheep-shaped mounds lying on the valley floor over which the glaciers passed. We are keen geography students. And one day, when we are thirsty, we discover a spring coming out of a rocky bank. We try the water and find it is fizzy, rusty-tasting and naturally carbonated.

We are always hungry. This is the downside of our lifestyle. We can't afford to eat properly and must stretch out our small allowance of *francs*. In the hostel, when no-one is around, we cut a thin slice off each of the started loaves belonging to other hostellers and hope they don't notice. Our packet of dried Knorr vegetable soup has to be stretched as far as possible, and so we dilute it with so much water and stale bread that it turns into an indigestible pudding. Eating poorly reduces our energy levels. As we walk one day along a mountain road towards the snow-covered peaks at the head of the valley, we pass a village rubbish dump where someone has deposited a load of old pears. We find a few that are edible and are enjoying them when we turn around and see a rat running over the heap. What indescribably horrible germs we may be ingesting!

Danny and Serge have not forgotten us. We are just settling down one night in our hostel dormitory when some car lights disturb us from the road outside. I am wearing a clinging brushed-nylon nightdress with a big hole in it. It is inherited from my mother, and I am hardly a glamorous sight.

Mary goes to the window. "Bridget, it's Danny and Serge. Be quiet. Come quickly." We peep out, hoping that the *aubergistes* are soundly asleep in their beds.

Danny is trying to climb the drainpipe, which is rattling ominously. "Brigitte, I cannot *keees* you!" he wails. His English is just about up to that. This is a true Romeo and Juliet situation. But they fail in their attempt and eventually drift away, leaving our reputations unsullied.

Unsupervised
Metz, 3–4 April 1964

"*Bonjour, Jean Luc. Marie et Brigitte ici.*" We have hitchhiked to Metz, in eastern France, and are telephoning the boys. We will spend the last day or two with them, and that evening they collect us in their car. Once we arrive at the youth hostel in the forest, we find, to our surprise, that it has no *aubergistes*. It is unsupervised in every way, and Jean Luc and Pierre have decided that it is an ideal location for a little *amour*.

This is awkward. We did enjoy their singing, and we shared their food. We'd driven with them into the mountains beyond Clermont-Ferrand, and improved our French a little in their company. But we are not in the mood to have the total French experience, and we are at their mercy, in a forest from which we'd find it hard to escape. This is troublesome. We argue. I lose my temper, and Pierre is irritated. Mary, whose diplomatic skills are superior to mine, manages to keep Jean Luc smiling, but it is clear that neither of us will give in to their plans. Next morning, as we drive away from the forest, Pierre is grumpy beside me in the car. I'm past caring. I just want the journey to end. They drop us off with no address-swapping. We won't forget the lovely songs they taught us, and we have a photo of them that we had taken earlier in Clermont-Ferrand when they were smiling. French *garçons*, handsome, dark-haired and musical, they may be, but we are glad to escape.

Two Shillings
London, 6 April 1964

A few days later, we are in Trafalgar Square, where we ask a passer-by to take our photograph with my camera. Two rained-on girls with sticks and overloaded rucksacks who have been to France and back. We have two shillings between us to get out of London and all the way to Hereford.

It is certain that we'll return. The whole visit has cost less than ten pounds between us, and Mary is brooding ideas for a geography study in the Vallée de Chaudefour. The photos I had taken along the way are placed, dated and fixed neatly in my album.

Despite the glamour and the enchanting singing of the *garçons*, we haven't fallen in love. Neither have we needed to battle them off with sticks or sprinkle them with pepper. If anything, we've fallen in love with the seductive tones of the French language and certainly that crispy bread with butter and peach jam.

To Cities
London, May 1964

Mary has a boyfriend in London, but even more important is the Rudolf Laban School of Dance. She and Chris are attending a course, and I want to go to watch them. It takes some skill to go there and back in a weekend, but we can do it in four hours if we get good lifts.

As usual, we are short of money but need to get around the city. We get onto an Underground train without a ticket, and when we leave we tell the official at the exit gate that we didn't have time to buy one. We had got on at a closer station so that we would then pay for a shorter journey. "Did you come down the escalator?" We say that we did. "There is no escalator at that station, young ladies." And he embarrasses us, threatening us with consequences if we do it in the future.

The other problem with London, as with all big cities, is getting onto the road out of town to start hitching home. The A40 is the road we need, towards Oxford and then Gloucester, and this means paying for a bus or the Underground to the furthest edge of the city. Going to London costs us a lot of money.

Mary and I are planning a weekend trip to Scotland. "Miss Hipwell will never know!" we assure each other. My uncle and three cousins live in Glasgow but we sign out for a nearby youth hostel. No-one is likely to check. We leave on a Friday afternoon along the A49 towards Shrewsbury, and then north along the A6. There is always a lorry to give us a lift, and we grind in second gear over Shap Pass between the Lake District mountains to the west and the Pennines to the east, arriving with a surprised Uncle Jimmy at midnight. He lives in a four-storey tenement, a widower with his three little boys. Nonchalant and charming, he gives Mary a silver whisky flask curved to fit into the back pocket of a pair of trousers as we leave on the Sunday. Two days to Scotland and back. The journey is successfully accomplished.

There is another source of income for budgeting students. As we receive train fares paid by our local authorities, we are learning that we can benefit from our travel expenses by hitchhiking.

"It's all very well for you, Bridget," my friends are wont to say. "You live so far away."

"That's just my good luck," I counter. "It is three hundred miles to Northumberland. Much further than where you live. They don't even ask me to show the tickets." By hitchhiking, I can keep all this money and add substantially to my income. It is not entirely straightforward, though, because whichever way I choose between Hereford and Newcastle I must cross the country from south-west to north-east. Any route means circumventing the Pennines. My choices are to go north to Carlisle and then east, or to cut through the conurbations of Lancashire and Yorkshire, or to wind my way through the urban sprawls of Birmingham and the Midlands. Networks of roads must be learned. Sometimes I might get stuck in conurbations and need to pay local transport to the edge of towns. But I don't often get lost. My sixpenny road maps show the way.

Dance
Hereford, June 1964

Chris and Mary are students of modern dance, learning at our college the techniques of Rudolf Laban and Martha Graham. They love all kinds of dancing. They would love to see flamenco. What about a visit to Spain?

3

Grasshoppers And Bullfights

Spain, France, summer 1964

"Eeeek, ouch, help…" We are shrieking and yelling as, every time we put a foot down on the hot asphalt of the road, a cloud of giant grasshoppers leaps away from us in unpredictable directions. Whichever way we dodge, more come from another side, and we jump wildly away, while with horrible scrunches we find ourselves stepping on brown, scaly bodies.

Never did we imagine that these giant grasshoppers would be our first welcome into Spain. Glamorous flamenco dancers, handsome matadors yes – but giant grasshoppers? Definitely not.

The blue Mediterranean Sea lies below us as we scatter the clouds of leaping insects. The road winds up and then down into Spain around hairpin bends such as we've never seen in the mountains of our own country. The heat blasts us. It is never as hot as this in England. We five lassies, English, Welsh and Scottish, are propelling ourselves forward with our long sticks and carrying our tents and sleeping blankets on our backs. "Yoicks – aagh" and unspellable sounds escape us as we struggle forward through the myriad insects.

"Blackberries," Mary cries out. "Are they like ours? Can we eat them?" The prickly strands are crossing our path and scratching our bare legs. We look carefully at the berries and taste them. There is no doubt. In July, in Spain, blackberries are ripe, whereas at home we wouldn't be able to eat them until at least August. Their juice is refreshing, and between plucking and sucking them, and leaping away from the grasshoppers, we slowly descend the arid mountain road into Spain: the remote and inaccessible country that is drawn in the western corner of Hereford Cathedral's *Mappa Mundi*.

***

IDEAS OF SPAIN
HEREFORD, JUNE 1964

What did we know about Spain? Almost nothing. Conversations like this have taken place in our rooms at college in the weeks before our departure.

"They have fiestas in the afternoon!"

"You mean siestas, when they sleep, and then they stay up long into the night?"

"Yes, to avoid the heat. It will be really hot."

"I love the heat," I say. I'm always longing to be truly warm.

"Maybe we'll find some flamenco dancing." Mary and Chris are enthusiastic.

"But there is bullfighting. It's cruel."

We all agree about this. It is hard to balance what we feel must be warm-hearted Spanish people with such deliberate cruelty.

"We don't have to go to a bullfight."

"True. But it is part of Spanish life."

"They drink lots of red wine, don't they?"

"Don't boys play the guitar and serenade girls peeping behind their fans on their balconies?"

"That's only in the theatre. It can't really be like that."

"Probably the girls are just like us these days."

"What about Spanish boys? Is it risky? Are they flirtatious?"

"We managed the boys in France," says Mary. "We can surely cope in Spain. Let's go. English boys are so dull."

We know little or nothing about Franco and the Civil War of our parents' generation.

Back and forth go our discussions. First one person agrees to go, and then another, and others drop out. In the end, four of us prepare for the journey. Tonie – who knows a little Latin, which may help with Spanish – Chris, Mary and me.

"*Habla usted inglés?*" Do you speak English? We learn a few Spanish phrases from Hugo's *Spanish in Three Months*.

"*Soy inglesa.*" I am an English girl. Tonie insists on "*Soy galesa.*" I am a Welsh girl. We learn to say Good Morning, Please and Thank You in Spanish, and some of us learn to count so that we can work out what things cost. We'll manage.

A popular song by singer Cliff Richard is humming in my

mind. He sings passionately about a red rose in Spanish Harlem, whose eyes as black as coal look down and start a fire in his soul so that he loses control. I don't really know where Spanish Harlem is, but I have the idea that Spain may be full of handsome men attracted by beautiful women. Not that my friends or I have eyes as black as coal, but you never know. Romance is always a possibility.

Ascari's Restaurant
Hereford, June 1964

The time is approaching. "You are going to Spain?" asks José Maria, the waiter in Hereford's Ascari restaurant. "I will help you!" He pulls out a paper napkin and writes a letter in Spanish that we can take to his family in the northern town of Santander. It translates like this:

> Calle Antonio Lopez 3, Estación Sanitaria, Santander
> Dear family: This girl lives in Hereford and is a friend of mine. Help her a little. She is very simpática and soon I will write to you with more news from here. If you invite her to eat, please take account that she is vegetariana. José Maria

On the back of the napkin, he gives us a little lesson in Spanish, writing out the verbs "to have", "to take" and "to be". Importantly he writes *No Toques* with double exclamation marks, which we take to mean Hands Off, and *tortilla de patatas*, a potato omelette, very useful for non-meat-eaters.

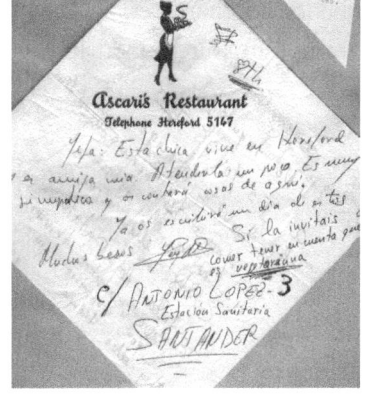

Armed with this information, we think we may find our way to Santander.

Two Pound Ferry Tickets
Hereford to Paris, 5–6 July 1964

We consider ourselves experienced hitchhikers who can cross the Channel to France with ease, Mary and I already having done it once at Easter time. I pair up with Chris, and Mary with Tonie. "See you in Paris tomorrow," we say as we split up, planning to meet in Laumière youth hostel.

After passing through London, Chris and I ride to Dover in an MG sports car, travelling on the A2 main road at 100 miles per hour. Only the best for the hitching girls from Hereford, we agree. At Dover, we spend the necessary £2 on our walk-on ferry boat fare to Calais. I decide to make a scrapbook of our travels when I get home, so from now on I take photos, collect postcards and paper items, and make daily notes.

With Tramps
Paris, 6–8 July 1964

It is simple to travel from the port of Calais to Paris. We reach the city in five and a half hours of hitching. The next day, while waiting for Mary and Tonie to catch up with us, Chris and I are attracted by the *louche* characters who hang around on the banks of the Seine, tramps and hitchhikers like us.

We buy bottles of cheap beer, and chat in whatever languages we have in common. At the youth hostel, we make friends with people from many nations, Germany, Canada, Tunisia. Two boys from Tunisia, Barbati Ahmed and Djebara Mohamed, write out all our names in beguiling Arabic script. They give us a locally printed newspaper dated 5 July 1964 and its Arabic equivalent, 25 June 1384. These are cultural riches indeed.

FRIENDLY FRENCH SUMMER
PARIS TO PERPIGNAN, 9–10 JULY 1964

When we leave, we reorganise the hitching. Tonie travels with a new Scottish friend called Maureen, Chris with Peter, an English boy, and I with Mary. We arrange to meet in Perpignan youth hostel, near the border with Spain. This is the friendly summer of 1964, where the sun shines and where lifts are easy in the relaxed land of France. Mary and I pass the first night in Lyon station's *salle d'attente*, the waiting room. On we go through Avignon, Nîmes, Montpellier and my first view and swim in the Mediterranean, to Perpignan.

The driver who takes us over the grassy dunes to the sea explains that the plantations along the coastal plain are *raisins*, which we gradually realise does not mean raisin bushes but vineyards.

They Really Speak Spanish
Portbou, 11–12 July 1964

We know there are fewer hostels in Spain than in France, and we are carrying two tents. Our packs are heavy in the heat as we cross the border into Spain among the giant grasshoppers.

At the very bottom of these parched brown hills, along the winding road we can see a little town, Portbou, the first in Spain. People are speaking Spanish. It is true, they really do. There is a public water fountain in the street where we can wash our hands and fill our water bottles.

We change some British pounds into *pesetas*. We have decided we can afford a simple meal in a restaurant, and the salad is inexpensive. "Salad, *por favor*," I say to the waiter. The others order *paella*, rice with fishy-looking objects in it, of no appeal to me, the vegetarian. When my salad comes, I am surprised to find it is a few sliced tomatoes drenched in olive oil. What, no lettuce? And as I've never seen olive oil before I am baffled. Does one lick it up? I'm doubtful. The waiter brings us some shell-shaped bread rolls, hard, heavy and dry, unlike the light crispy baguettes we have eaten in France.

"*Qué va à beber?*" asks the waiter. What would you like to drink? We don't know about wine, coming from Britain. Beer, yes, or stout, or cider from the Herefordshire orchards, but we are not used to wine. "*Vino tinto*," he encourages us. We agree, and for a couple of *pesetas* we drink a little glass of strong red wine each, which causes us to grimace and then grin at each other.

Evening is falling. We head uphill from the town and pitch our two tiny tents under some olive trees. I am nodding off in the tent. "Aaaagh – help – aaaagh…" Chris is shrieking beside me. What has happened? She scrambles towards the opening, dragging her blanket, knocking into the sides of the tent, hysterical, tearful. She shakes the blanket, and the biggest, ugliest giant grasshopper ever known flits out and away. It had found its way in beside her sleepy body, flapping as it tried to escape, terrifying her, trapped as she was in the folds of the blanket. I am laughing, which is unforgiveable. It had been worse than a nightmare. Later, during the night, we have more unwanted visitors. Some young men had watched us as we came up the hill from the restaurant. "*No, no, señores,*" we say in our best Spanish. They eventually go away, but tomorrow we will find a campsite where with luck we will be safe from both human and insect predators.

THE EASY SEA
SANT MIQUEL, 13–16 JULY 1964

The sea is warm in Sant Miquel, the next little town along the coast. Warm sea water? Surely it is not possible? In Tonie's home county of Pembrokeshire, the water is always cold, and in Northumberland where my family live it is perishing all year round. But here we strip down completely bare and soak ourselves in the salty water, loafing and laughing, and playing at being mermaids.

Chris has fallen ill with Spanish sickness, and therefore we decide to stay and rest in Sant Miquel for a couple of days. We eat Spanish bread, walk among the cactus plants and bamboo canes that line the tracks, and cool ourselves in the sea. Our backs and shoulders become sore and blistered from sunburn. We've never known heat like this before.

"*Si, señoritas. Muy barato.*" It is very cheap, young ladies, to hire my boat, says the young man by the beach. Chris, Mary and I have used oars on boating ponds in parks in England. We'll certainly manage here in Spain. We take turns rowing out into the bay on the calm water, enjoying our skill, admiring the attractive situation of

Sant Miquel, with its orange rooftops and church spire surrounded by steep brown mountains.

This is perfection. We have never been so happy. But then we notice the line of a strong current in the smooth surface of the sea and find that we are unable to avoid it. The current pulls our rowing boat into itself, and we are being swept out to sea, towards Africa. Rowing madly, we struggle against the pull of the current, but it is really strong. Somehow, we steer the little boat as far as a rocky outcrop on the northern edge of the bay, where the waves throw the boat onto a rock, crashing us forward and sucking us back again. We try to turn the boat back towards the beach, losing an oar in the process, and now the boat begins to spin around. We think we'll leap out onto the rock, but only Chris manages to do so, leaving Mary and me alone in the boat.

With great effort, with the single oar, we coax the boat back towards the harbour. Chris has been left behind on her isolated rock, a long way from the village. We return the boat to its bewildered owner, minus one oar, and then scramble along the rocks to find her. Our feet are sore from the jagged rocks, but we are together again. This has been nothing like the boating ponds at home.

SEPARATING
CALATAYUD, 17 JULY 1964

As we nibble our breakfast bread beside the tents, Tonie says, "Maureen and I have decided to head back home. We like Spain, but it is too hot. And we don't want to carry those heavy rucksacks. We're returning to France, where it is cooler, and then we'll get back home."

Tonie is never happy when she is far from Wales. Maureen too is ready to return with her. This means that they will travel back along the roads through France, north to Paris and then over the English Channel. We know that they will manage it easily enough.

"*Adiós, amigas,*" we say. Goodbye, friends. Mary, Chris and I will head south via Madrid to Andalusia, a further journey of a thousand kilometres. The ways are uncertain, unknowable, but that is what we will do, three fair-haired unaccompanied English girls with a tiny budget. My notes reappear later in my scrapbook:

We passed through Barcelona, Lérida, Zaragoza where we washed and refreshed at the home of some hospitable Spaniards, crossed the wild Aragon fruit country, hitched, hitched, to Calatayud. Here we were entertained to a lunch of little red crayfish and *vino* by some students from Zaragoza. After lunch we swam in the local *piscina*, having a welcome and necessary wash.

One of the students, Raphael, takes us to his flat. My scrapbook:

On top of a hill overlooking the town at night, Mary and Pedro danced in and out of the trees, Chris and Frederico were otherwise engaged, and I sat enraptured by Raphael's singing and guitar playing. It was romantic until the midges started biting. We slept for a few hours at the flat and left at 6 am next morning.

Danger
Bailén, 18 July 1964

One lift takes us all the way to Madrid, and from there we find the road heading south. We are offered a lift in a large van in which the sectioned-off back is entirely windowless. Too shy to demur, we accept their offer. Several men and at least one woman are enclosed with us in the complete darkness. We can't share more than a couple of words of Spanish with them, are completely disoriented in the noisy van and don't know how far we are going or in what direction. We have wild unspoken fears that they might be planning to sell us to a white slave trader or something worse.

The van stops, finally, and we tumble out onto the bank of a rushing green river. Here our co-travellers encourage us to dip ourselves in the cooling water, which seems dangerously fast-flowing. The woman, we notice, is pregnant, and the tall driver appears to be her husband. Together with the three dark-haired young men passengers, they lay out a picnic on the river bank, sharing it unquestioningly with the three English girls they have

picked up. Why did we worry? They are generous and kind.

From there, we head south through the landscape which is arid and dry. We find ourselves walking past a rural scene where people are raking and thrashing mounds of golden corn, straw and chaff, and donkeys are turning wheels. It is a harvest picture from biblical times.

A Jaguar with a British numberplate stops. "We can take you as far as Valdepeñas," says a man with a cut-glass English voice. We climb into the back seat. Surely this can't be true. English businessmen? Their umbrellas and bowler hats are lying on the rack behind us. As the car drives south, we admire the glorious sunset sky over to the west, and the mountains lit up by a lightning storm.

After the Jaguar, we are picked up by a lorry heading for our destination of Córdoba. This is great good luck. We should be there by the early morning. As midnight approaches, we reach the point where the road turns west towards Córdoba, near the town of Bailén.

"*Una feria*," says the lorry driver. A fair! We see the lights and the cheerful crowds of people, and call out, "Stop, please stop!" Our plans have changed at this very moment. A Spanish fiesta – this is exactly what we have been hoping to see in Andalusia, in the south of Spain.

We launch ourselves into the gaiety of the scene, fairground rides, families, chatter, noise and excitement. The young men of the town soon realise that some English *señoritas* have appeared out of nowhere. They are smiling, charming, and pay for us to go on the various rides. We are having a wonderful time, laughing and enjoying ourselves. At last, we realise how tired we are. A quiet spot is what we need, to put up our tent and rest for the night. We bid the boys farewell, but they don't seem to understand, or want to. Walking out of town along the road towards Córdoba, we pass the last street lights into the complete darkness of the countryside. But we are not alone. Ten or a dozen boys are following us. Never mind, we reassure each other. We are strong girls, with big, long sticks, and we think that we can outwalk these short young men. They crowd round us as we walk, talking assertively in Spanish and becoming increasingly annoying. They start to manhandle us, hurting our blistered, sunburned shoulders. No matter how we remonstrate, they are persistent. We walk faster and faster and begin to leave some of them behind. Those who are still with us become more aggressive. Then the trouble seems more serious because two or three of them had returned to the town and are now passing ahead of us on their motor scooters. We are trapped. We aren't safe walking forward or backward.

One of the young men on a scooter talks to us in a few words of English. He encourages us to get on behind him. He is trying to explain that he will take us back to the town. Somehow, we have a sense that he is a little more trustworthy than the others, although we cannot be sure. We ask if he will take us to the *Policía*, where we think we will be safe, and he seems to agree. Thus, with our rucksacks on our backs and sticks in our hands, each of us climbs on the back of one of the motor scooters, clinging to the drivers, who turn the vehicles round, leaving the rest of the boys behind on the road. Even as we are going, I am unsure if he will really take us to the safety of the *Policía*. We are completely at the mercy of these scooter boys, and as we ride I find myself mumbling some incoherent prayers.

The boys, however, are conscientious and have spoken truly. They drop us off by a large building in which there are some green-uniformed *Guardia Civil*, the military policeman. We have seen these policemen before with their green cloaks and three-cornered hats, machine guns at their sides, and expect to be safe with them. Being used to British policemen, who are usually on the side of victims, we have no reason to think otherwise in Spain. Not at first, anyway. Long explanations and gesticulations take place between the boys and the guards. We are frightened and exhausted. The guards indicate that we may place our blankets on the floor in the corridor, where we can sleep.

However, it seems that the *Guardia Civil* also think that unprotected English girls are available for their pleasure. All through the night, we fight their attentions with difficulty but with determination. These men, like the boys from the fairground, seeing us travelling alone, in the dark of the night, don't know how to interpret us. We get through the night with obstinate resistance. We have survived the danger.

Beauty And The Bullfight
Córdoba, 19–22 July 1964

In the morning, we escape with relief. Our fears are left behind us as one lift after another takes us closer to Córdoba, passing through miles of orange-tree plantations and olive groves.

Córdoba is the last city in Spain on Hereford's *Mappa Mundi*, at the *Terminus Europe*, where it is drawn as a large tower with a red dome. Now we are there, three twentieth-century girls travelling the same routes as pilgrims from hundreds of years ago.

The white-walled narrow streets of this town enchant us. Finally, we have arrived in the Spain that we imagined – parching hot weather, parks where children ride their little tricycles along palm-tree shaded paths, orange trees with flowers and fruit at the same time, glimpses into flower-filled patios, quiet afternoons where everyone disappears for the siesta, and no visitors except ourselves.

We find a *pension*, which costs us five shillings a night, not much more than the cost of a youth hostel at home. In the morning, we look down from our window over an enormous heap of golden melons for sale in the square. In Britain, a melon is a luxury, but here, in Spain, we can buy a delicious ripe and juicy fruit for ninepence, less than the price of a cup of tea.

We observe how women use fans, opening them with a flick of the wrist. In the marketplace, we buy our own. Whisking a cooling draught over our faces is a pleasurable sensation in the heat, and so practical. And we buy straw sombreros, more usually seen on men than women, to enjoy the shade over our eyes.

A woman has arranged heaps of different kinds of pottery on the ground. There is a special water pot we have been looking out for. People hold them in the air, aiming a spout of water confidently into their open mouths. Everyone can drink from them without their mouths touching the pot. It is such a good idea, so hygienic and sensible. We each buy a small *agua pot*, as we call them, and resolve to educate our British compatriots at home about their use.

"*Pss pss, Rubia,*" the men hiss. Everywhere we go, they leer at us as they pass in the streets and from the doorways of the bars. We deduce that *Rubia* means Blonde Girl. We can't escape this attention. When two students, Pepe and Pichichi, make friends with us, we are glad to have their company as this ensures us a kind of peace. We wander with them under the orange trees that line the streets, and try to reach a fruit. We can't understand why no-one steals and eats the oranges, but the boys tell us they are *agria*, which means bitter, and the trees are ornamental.

Our friendly students take us to the Mezquita. Never have we seen such a wonder. We know that the Arabs had been in Spain, and had been driven out, but little more than that. This is their mosque, which is now being used as a Catholic church. Rows and rows of internal double arches, mounted on slender pillars, golden stone alternating with red brick, range back into the darkness, where we can easily imagine the Moorish men of old among the shadows. Later, the boys take us into the Alcázar, the palace of the Christian kings. They tell us that it was built on Roman and Arab foundations. Green plants grow against the tall Moorish-looking walls with their pointed crenellations, and they show us round some Roman baths that are being excavated.

In the city, donkeys are pulling carts along narrow alleys where flowers hang from balconies, tiny churches are at the ends of little squares with fountains and crosses. People are going about their daily business. This is the Spain we've been looking for.

There is one decision to make. Will we, or not? We decide that we will. My scrapbook:

At Córdoba we went to our first bullfight after having seen one on television the night before. What did we think of it? Cruel? Yes, but not as bad as we had expected and all is over in twenty minutes. Exciting? Yes, if the matadors are good. Otherwise it becomes a series of endless deaths. Skilful? Definitely, and demanding much courage from the matadors. Dangerous? Quite. Several matadors received minor injuries while we were watching, and most professional bullfighters die in the ring. It is always fatal for the poor bull. For the tourists? Not only for them. Most of the people at our bullfight were Spanish.

What did we think of it? We couldn't say we exactly enjoyed it, but it was an experience of an important part of Spanish life. And what do Spanish people say if you tell them you think it is cruel?

They say – yes, perhaps it is cruel, but it is a fight between man and beast, brains against strength.

As we had travelled through Spain, we had seen huge advertisements in the shape of a big black bull with white horns for Brandy Veterano. I obtain a booklet in English to stick in my scrapbook. This describes in great detail the history and techniques of bullfighting. It says: "The spectacle of bullfighting, so traditional in Spain, is most beautiful and exciting when truly understood and properly performed." Thirty-two pages of explanation and vocabulary follow.

The most famous of all Spanish matadors at this time is El Cordobés, and I buy a postcard of him. He is walking towards the camera, holding a red cloak in his left hand, in front of his fancy bloodstained costume. I also find a newspaper article of him and his wife at the christening of their baby. She is prettily dressed in a white lacy mantilla. They are a picture of Spanish good looks and romanticism. I save both items for my scrapbook.

Despite my notes, the impression I have, to this day, is of the bull trotting innocently into the ring. The gate was opened, and the animal was being directed forward, unknowingly. All the humans participating in the spectacle know what is going to happen to it while the creature does not. It is not a vicious beast with wicked intent. That element is supplied by the human imagination. It will only react to what is being done to it. Then, at the end, it is degradingly dragged from the ring though the sawdust. Despite what I wrote then, I cannot justify this aspect of human nature.

VILLAGE
CÓRDOBA, 23 JULY 1964

"*Señor, stop, por favor!*" The driver who has given us a lift in his car is puzzled. "*Aqui? Por que? No hay nada aqui!*" Here? Why? There's nothing here.

We are out in the countryside near Córdoba and have seen a village a short distance from the road. We want to investigate. We are endlessly curious about rural life where the animals and crops are so different from those in Britain.

As we approach, we see low, white-painted houses with red-tiled roofs, the walls covered with pots of flowers. A plump, tall teenage girl appears and we engage in conversation using our dozen words of Spanish.

"*Inglesas!*" She understands and smiles, and her mother appears in the doorway of their house. We exchange names. She is called Maria, and likes Mary's pronunciation of her name in English. Soon children and neighbouring women appear. Because we are friendly and curious, they nod as we indicate that we'd like to wander around between their houses. We admire the well for the animals, learning that a donkey turns the wheel, bringing up the water, which runs into a long trough. Another well is for drinking water, and here a bucket is lowered and raised by human hands. We see pigs grunting as they roam freely around. Their pigsty is made of brushwood. A goat is resting in a shade created by a flat piece of metal fixed in the corners onto tall sticks. Like the pigs, the other farm creatures all seem to wander freely. They know where they belong.

We head out to the fields past a tall hedge of spiny cactus. A hedge made of cactus! In Britain, ours are made of prickly hawthorn. Ahead are some great pyramidal straw stacks piled where the men have been threshing. As we approach, the men are leaving for their midday break. They are tall, thin and suntanned, their heads shaded from the searing heat by straw sombreros. A man and a boy are seated on sacks on the back of a *burro*, a long-eared, patient donkey, guiding it by a simple rope halter. They are surprised to see us, but Maria chatters to them in Spanish, explaining that we have just appeared in their village. They see that we are fascinated by the *burro*, and jump down so that Chris and I may be seated on its back and Mary takes our photograph. We always use our small supply of films cautiously, but this village is going to be our priority.

Back at Maria's house, the family invites us to share the midday meal. We are seated with them around a wooden table in the cool, shady room. A huge bowl containing big yellow peas and chopped vegetables is placed in the middle of the table. Everyone is given a spoon and we all eat from the same bowl. It certainly makes a lot less washing-up, and we think it is a good system. The peas, we learn, are called *garbanzos*. They are yellow and crunchy. I manage to avoid eating the small pieces of meat. We are being treated with dignity and kindness.

Probably this is the first time these villagers have met English people, and they are as curious about us who have turned up from nowhere as we are about them and their lifestyle. It doesn't seem so bad to us, to live in the sunshine, to produce your own food and to share a close family life. After the meal we ask them in our inadequate Spanish, "*Desea fotografia?*" Would you like us to take your photograph?

With many *si, si, señoritas*, the family assembles outside the curtained doorway of their little white house: short sturdy grandmother; small bony grandfather; Maria; two tall, thin grown-up sons; and the youngest son with his puppy. We can see that the younger generation is taller than the older. Perhaps they've had better food. Before long, more villagers appear, and the next group photograph is of twenty-five people, eight of whom are healthy, smiling children. Then the women call out, "*Los hombres, solo los hombres*," which we realise means we must take a photo of the men by themselves. We oblige. My scrapbook does not record that later I posted these photos to the villagers, but I hope, and expect, that I did.

BREAKFAST
SEVILLE, 24–25 JULY 1964

"*Si, señoritas, residencias muy bonitas,*" says the matronly lady at the *pensión* in Seville. Beautiful rooms. She takes us up a flight of stairs and we come out on a balcony around an open, flower-filled courtyard. Doors to the different rooms lead off the balcony, and she allows us to choose. This is bliss, and we take one overlooking the street. Leaving our bags, we wander off through the *Calle del Flores* and other narrow streets where the houses are close together providing maximum shade from the sun. My scrapbook:

The heat is scorching. Even the wind is hot. In Seville, near the cathedral, we ran into Henrico, a Norwegian boy we had met in Córdoba. Chris and I sat with him, fanning ourselves, in the cathedral square for the rest of the day. It was too expensive for us to go in, and we were too exhausted by the heat to move. Mary somehow managed to get in for half price. But we found no flamenco dancing in Seville. It's too hot for the tourists in summer, Henrico said.

We'll have to come back at a different time of year, we agree.

Chris draws Mary and me to our window in the cool of the early next morning. Children are carrying parcels wrapped in newspaper, and there are enticing smells. We go down and follow them to a house in a dark alley. A plump woman dressed in black is sitting in front of a large pot of boiling oil, into which she is squirting what looks like pancake mixture as one might pipe icing on a cake. She makes a spiral pattern that fills the surface of the boiling oil. When the mixture is golden brown she lifts the spiral out, cutting it with scissors into variously sized pieces and dipping them in sugar. She wraps them up in paper, hands them over and takes a few coins in exchange. We buy some. We've never tasted anything like them, so crispy, crunchy, sweet and hot.

MILESTONES NORTH
BURGOS, 26 JULY 1964

We have a destination in Santander, the contact written on the napkin by our Spanish waiter friend in Hereford, José Maria. Perhaps his family will welcome us. Santander is over four hundred miles to the north, but we plan an overnight hitchhiking expedition. Certainly we are optimistic. My scrapbook:

Left Córdoba with much regret on Sunday morning. Where were we going? To Santander, right on the northernmost Atlantic coast of Spain. Why? We wanted to visit the north of Spain, and El Cordobés was to be fighting there the following evening. We didn't know if we'd ever get there in time.

First we get lifts eastward as far as Bailén, the town of unpleasant memories. Once there, the main road heads north towards Madrid, and we realise that there are milestones marked with the distance to Madrid once every kilometre. M 240 means Madrid is 240 kilometres further. The next one shows M 239, the next M 238 and so on. As we are interested in the agriculture and crops in the landscape, we make a spontaneous decision to do a land-use survey of all the fields through which we are passing, as far as Madrid and further if possible. Notebooks in hand, we write the number on the milestones, recording olive groves and maize plantations, and as the road passes through arid semi-desert mountains we record that too. My scrapbook:

After Madrid, lifts became more difficult. We crossed the mountains north of the capital by moonlight, still continuing our land-use survey, and reached Burgos by 3 am. No more lifts were forthcoming, so we slept – accompanied by various police-type men and local musicians on the pavement – until 6 am when we got our first lift, crossing the Cantabrian mountains to reach Santander by midday.

In twenty three hours we had crossed almost the whole of Spain, a total distance of nearly 700 kilometres, or 450 miles, and it had not cost us a *peseta*.

We carefully store our notebooks with the land-use survey in our packs. We have passed from the brown lands of olive plantations into the greener north where fields of maize are waiting to be harvested. We plan that once back in college, we will make a full-scale chart illustrating all the different crops and land-use as part of our final-year geography presentations. We really are serious students.

Different Spain
Santander, 27–28 July 1964

"*Cuánto cuesta un billete?*" we ask at the bullring. How much is a ticket? We had arrived just in time, but even the cheapest tickets in the hot sun are 300 *pesetas*, well beyond our resources. That idea must be abandoned, but we have our other destination. My scrapbook:

We visited the family of José Maria, the Spanish boy we'd met in Hereford. We arrived in the middle of their lunch, looking not at all smart in our raggedy clothes. They didn't appear to mind and invited us to lunch the following day. Then one of José Maria's brothers, Javier, and his friends took us out in the bay in their boat.

Santander has a lovely beach with sunbathing visitors, and fishing boats along the harbour. From the boat, we could see green peninsulas around the bay and the Isla de Pedrosa. The boys have perfect manners, and Javier is politely encouraging and friendly. I begin to fall in love with him. He is so dark and handsome.

I have shown José Maria's family the letter on the table napkin that he had written to them in the Hereford restaurant. His words and handwriting are a link between him, us and them. This is a well-to-do family. They encourage us to go to Santillana del Mar, a nearby town with traditional local architecture, and near the prehistoric cave paintings in Altamira.

Cave Paintings
Santillana del Mar, 29 July–4 August 1964

Mary and Chris pack up the tent in the campsite where we have spent the night, and hitchhike to Santillana del Mar. I decide to walk the twenty miles to wear out my feelings at leaving Javier behind. On the way, while swimming in an inland rivulet of the sea, some friendly Spanish girls approach me.

"Eat with us, English girl," they say. I am taken to their house, where I am given a three-course meal: tomato salad with onions, haricot bean soup, fried eggs and finally fruit. This helps to sober down my whirling emotions. Leaving them, as I approach Santillana I am looking out for our agreed signal of orange flags. There it is, tacked onto the prickly cactuses of the roadside – Mary's orange shirt. I know she and Chris are camping behind the hedge.

We visit the original cave paintings of Altamira which are open to visitors. The red and black paintings of bison, bulls and other animals are etched onto the walls of the caves. We breathe deeply in the shadows of the caverns where our human ancestors had sheltered and painted as long ago as 12,000 bc. We have no understanding that the moisture from our breath might be damaging the paintings.

At the campsite, we play at being three little maids from school, from Gilbert and Sullivan's *The Mikado*. Despite being in Spain rather than Japan, we ask our new friends, two boys both called Bernard, to take a photo.

Mary and Chris go for rides with the Bernards on their motor scooters. I am lamenting for Javier, but it is no use. We visit him and his family again as we leave Santillana, passing through Santander on our way east. But his dark eyes and soulful gazes are for someone else.

No Services
To the frontier, 5–7 August 1964

Now we must leave Spain. My scrapbook:

We followed the coast road for a while, great rocky scenery, silver bays and *rias*. And then into the Cantabrian scene of high forested mountains. Once we were away from the sea, the land was hot, bare and desert-like again. On we went until we reached Pamplona. Here we shared our room with two French girls, also hitchhiking. Next day we headed for the border. We started well by walking for two hours round the ring road of Pamplona and ending up near where we started!

Along the way, we persuade a passer-by to take a photo of us. Decorated with cowbells, sombreros, our *agua pots*, sticks, a brush made of palm leaves, and bearing our loaded rucksacks, the blurry photograph shows us setting off homeward, thumbs up, with big smiles on our faces.

Si, si, we may camp in their fields *por la noche*, for the night, agrees the friendly countrywoman at a farm in the foothills of the Pyrenees. There is a great conical pointed strawstack in the field of stubbly maize stalks where we place our tent. In order not to contaminate the field, we ask them to show us *los servicios*, the toilets. Embarrassed gestures follow. Vague waving towards the fields. It takes us a while to understand that we must find our own private spots. Certainly, we have used many smelly primitive facilities throughout our travels in Spain, but here we are really back to basics. Mother Earth will receive our offerings direct.

As we approach the frontier, we have the bittersweet feeling of parting. We are leaving the warmth of Spain for cooler, damper lands. My scrapbook:

> *We camped in the woods, cooked a last Spanish meal and lay chattering and peacefully reminiscing when it started to pour with rain. It got worse, so we thought we'd better move, in the process of which I added to my miseries by falling waist high in a stream. After penetrating black woods with our torch (the battery was almost gone) we reached the protection of the frontier guards. After feeding us, and offering us shelter, they offered us a last souvenir of Spain. We refused. We slept our final night in Spain on the wooden floor of a nearby shop.*

Once over the border, we must separate. Chris needs to go home, and Mary and I are heading for the Massif Central, where we had been at Easter. We want to see the people we'd made friends with before. She is thinking about doing her geography special study, our final-year dissertation, in France.

We assemble by the road for our journey north.

"*Dónde va usted?*" Chris asks the driver in her best Spanish. Where are you going, sir?

"I'm going as far as London, if that is of interest," replies the driver in perfect English. This is almost unbelievable. Here is a lift that will take her all the way through France and over the sea to London. We wave her off, and then direct ourselves towards central France.

French Days
Chambon, 10–22 August 1964

"*S'il vous plaît,*" says the man driving an ice cream van, indicating small spaces beside the driving wheel. He gives us a lift to Bordeaux, where we arrive at midnight. As well as feeding us with ice cream, he allows us to sleep in his van overnight. The next night we are extravagant and spend the money to stay in Clermont-Ferrand youth hostel before leaving for Chambon in the mountains. It is so easy to hitchhike our way around in France.

Mary and I dance and sing with Danny and Serge and other glamorous young French people in Chambon. We stay at the barn opposite the youth hostel. My scrapbook:

> *Spent many happy days seeing old friends, making new ones, sleeping in the sun, having picnics in the woods, climbing trees, having parties in barns, making jam from wild redcurrants, visiting nightclubs and casinos, sleeping in barns, learning French songs and dances, eating St Nectaire cheese and local butter, going to an international folklore festival, buying sabots from the sabotière in Chambon, having my United Nations' birthday party at the youth hostel, with cake, wine, cheese, and even sometimes doing some geography...*

Summer Is Fading
Paris and Brittany, 22 August–1 September 1964

Towards the end of the month, we make our way to Paris again. Mary then hitchhikes home to England while I head for Brittany because I don't yet feel like going back to England. Here I make friends with the Berthelot family in the village of Saint-Gilles-Pligeaux. They speak their own Breton language in preference to French. I sleep in the barn, learn to milk cows by hand, and observe the methods of farming and haymaking. My scrapbook:

> *One day, as I lay dreaming beside a lake in Brittany, I decide to count my money. Twelve French francs, about eighteen shillings. I thought, "I'd better go home soon." So next day I packed my bag and hitchhiked to Boulogne via Rouen. Crossed to Dover and saw the channel swimmer. Rode in a Jaguar to London and came home on an overnight train.*

As easy as that! My scrapbook doesn't say how I had the money for the train but probably I took it out from my post office account once in England.

Back Home
Newcastle, 3 September 1964

I open the back door of my terraced house in Newcastle, and my father laughs at me.

"Bridget, we must have a photo of this!" he says. He stands me by the wall in our back lane. I'm smiling, healthy-looking, wearing my sombrero from Spain, leaning on my strong stick and carrying a long loaf of French bread for my family, who have never seen such a thing.

From 5 July until 3 September, there have been two months of travel on a pittance and through a world of drama. Leaping away from giant grasshoppers on the Mediterranean coast, south to Andalusia and then to the cooler north of Spain, we've mingled with the people of what to us is an unknown and exotic land. Orange trees and olive groves, fans and *agua pots*, siestas and fiestas, gorgeous boys, menacing gangs and aggressive policemen, farming families, melons and red wine, hot weather, bullfights and the lovely white lanes of Córdoba. None of us has found a romantic man whose eyes look down into our soul. True love has yet to be found. And neither have we encountered flamenco. This time, anyway.

We've experienced first-hand the macho culture and shared a bowl of food with a rural family. We've been drawn to the simplicity of farming life without spending enough time to understand the hardships that lay behind it. The glamour has pulled us, and reality has educated us, a little. But surely we'll return, and to France as well. The gals of Hereford College are getting nifty at hitting the road.

4

Roads In The North

Hereford, autumn 1964

"Let's see if we can get away with it," says Mary. Our end-of-course special studies must be agreed with our geography lecturer Mr Thompson.

"Who would want to study Swindon?" says Mary. We are expected to research geographical development in our home areas. I share her reluctance. My family lives in Northumberland, which is far away, my parents are not getting on and the atmosphere at home is gloomy. It would be much more fun to do our studies in France, with captivating landscapes, French boys and crispy bread with peach jam.

We approach Mr Thompson and assemble our arguments. "We can do a comparison with the North Wales glaciated landscape and the Vallée de Chaudefour," Mary says.

I add my own perspective. "I visited Brittany in the summer. There are similar granite landscapes in Cornwall, and the Breton language is related to Cornish."

Mr Thompson is surprised. He gazes at us kindly. No-one else has made such requests. "And what about the language? How good is your French?"

Here we bluster. "We are studying French," we say. "We can look at the maps in the mayors' offices."

"It is expensive to travel to France. And where will you stay?"

This is easy to answer. We have become expert hitchhikers by this time. "It costs nothing to hitchhike, and the only cost is the ferry from Dover to Calais," we say. "There are youth hostels in France too, where it is cheap to stay."

Mr Thompson knows about youth hostels, but he doesn't realise that we are more likely to ask farmers if we can sleep in their barns instead, which costs us nothing.

He decides not to push the matter further. "If you are really sure…"

"Of course we are," we declare, and leave him, feeling gleeful that we have got our way. Now our work will mean more journeys to France, North Wales and Cornwall. The hitchhiking girls of Hereford College will be putting their travelling skills to good academic purpose.

***

Shivering
Northern England, New Year 1965

In the cold, wintry days after Christmas, Mary is hitchhiking with a tall, long-legged thin student friend from Rhodesia. Arlene is used to the best of everything. She is privileged, intolerant, with servants to wait on her every wish. They arrive in Newcastle, where I am at home for the winter break. The tall house in which I live with my mother and father, brothers and sisters is full of silent gloom. We manage to exchange presents and eat Christmas fare, but the atmosphere is loaded with tension between my parents. There are dreamlike images in my mind, unwilling to be brought into the light.

Mary and I are at Whitley Bay at a New Year party in the smart

Rex Hotel. We are dancing and the air is hot and stuffy. "We'll cool off in the sea," we decide, and run down to the beach, stripping off completely naked. Letting our clothes drop by the sea wall, we run pink and bare down to the waves. And we shriek and scream and duck ourselves in the shockingly cold water. Hysterically laughing, unable to take any more, we run back up the beach in the icy darkness. "There they are, two girls." An audience has gathered, pretending not to watch as we pull our resisting clothes over our sandy bodies, all lit up by the lights along the promenade.

It is always about surviving the cold. We hitchhike to the Lake District, which is beautiful during the winter. In Borrowdale youth hostel, at bedtime, we fill up our hot water bottles in the kitchen. They are an essential winter accessory. We shiver under the heavy woollen ex-army blankets on our two-tier iron bunks, the metal cold as stone. Fully clothed, unmoving and stiff, we try to retain the warmth of our bodies in a cocoon under the grey weight. Our hot water bottles heat the damp blankets and create steam, which filters out as little clouds in the cold air around us.

In the morning, Mary and I manage to rob a little lard from one of the other hosteller's food supplies and fry our stale bread with onions that we have brought from home. Onion sandwiches for breakfast are surprisingly filling. This is all too much for Arlene, who is used to the warmth and luxuries of her native land, and she leaves us, hitchhiking alone back to Hereford. Mary and I make our way up the Borrowdale valley. Our path leads us to the road that turns north into Honister Pass. Then follows a long uphill climb. Near the summit, we find a working slate mine and quarry. We approach the sound of hammering that we hear coming from a shed, and no-one stops us from investigating. Some men are at work sawing great slabs of rock, and with hammer and chisel they neatly split the greenish blocks into flat slates of different sizes. These are the famous Skiddaw slates, and their uses include rooftop slates, which we have seen on the farmhouses and cottages round about.

Our map shows us a path into the hills, and we climb up higher to Fleetwith Pike at 648 feet. From here we are looking northward. Stretching ahead is the U-shaped valley of Buttermere Lake, the steep mountainsides descending right to the water's edge. We know that the valley has been formed by glaciers cutting through the landscape and leaving streams hanging over the steep sides which tumble down as waterfalls. Scots pines, shapely and strong, frame the southern edge of the lake.

It is time for our lunch. We have some stale bread and margarine sandwiches, and two sweets to share. They are liquorice allsorts, cubes made of black liquorice with pink sugary layers. Their advantage is that the layers can be separated and shared, rather like the slates being split at the quarry. With a drink of cold water, we eat our tasty lunch, overlooking one of the most beautiful views in the land. We are rich.

Our Mothers Too
The Netherlands, Easter 1965

"It is a shame that our parents haven't travelled like us," Mary and I often say to each other. We are now experienced hitchhikers in foreign lands, having been first to France and then to Spain. Yet neither of our mothers has been overseas. If we can do it, why can't they?

"The country my mother would most like to visit," says Mary, "is the Netherlands. Some of her ancestors were Dutch."

The Netherlands? Holland, as we usually call it, doesn't have the tempting appeal of southern Europe, with its hot sunny weather, palm trees, wine and oranges growing on trees. Rather, it has windmills, waterways, flat countryside, red football-shaped cheeses, tulips, people wearing clogs. But it is closer, more achievable.

"I can't imagine my mother hitchhiking," I say, and neither can Mary. There is well-organised public transport in Holland, however, and we start to hatch our separate plans. The country has many youth hostels, and Mary's family has friends where her parents could be accommodated.

Mary intends to make her parents a gift and contacts a travel agency. She negotiates the cost of travel tickets, which must be paid for out of her student grant. The travel agent agrees that she may pay half the cost straight away and the rest over an ensuing period of time. When Mary tells her parents that she has done this, her mother breaks down in tears. "She cried all over the Christmas holiday," says Mary.

"Why was she sad?" I ask.

"She was overwhelmed with happiness because she couldn't believe that I could be so generous," Mary tells me.

"I'll come too and look after our mother," says my twelve-year-old brother Stephen in Newcastle. I am far away in Hereford, but together we organise things, and our mother buys a flight with British United Air Ferries, which will take her from Newcastle to Amsterdam for eighteen pounds and sixteen shillings. That is a big extravagance, and Stephen and I must go more cheaply by land and sea. My cheerful little brother starts to write a holiday notebook:

> *My train left precisely on time over the network of points outside Newcastle Central Station, into a new world. I was in a compartment with two young men who smoked happily away in my carefully chosen No Smoking compartment. The train stopped for breath only twice on the whole journey, at Durham and Doncaster. I enjoyed my 250 mile ride tremendously.*

He is to be met by our grandmother. His notebook:

> *I got to London five minutes early, at ten past twelve. I realised that Gran would not be at the station until one o'clock, so I had a good wander around King's Cross, seeing*

the lay of the land. At one o'clock Gran and I walked out of the station, and caught the 14 bus, then the 38 bus, and then the local train to Croydon, and the number 12 bus on the homing stretch to Gran's house.

Our grandmother is seventy-three years of age, a widow who has lived alone for over twenty years. She has prepared her quiet suburban house for my brother and me, two hungry, energetic young people, to be fed and given beds. She won't see her daughter, our mother, this time because we are travelling separately. My brother's notebook:

The next morning saw us hitching down to Dover. It took four lifts to get out of London. Three more lifts got us to Dover by about 1 pm, in a Cortina, a Mini and the last a tomato wagon.

We set sail with a few wispy clouds scudding along and a strong wind behind them. We went to Calais because Bridget wanted to have another look at France, and I wanted to see it because I have never seen it before, or anywhere else abroad for that matter. Fitting poem,

> *They went to see in a boat, a boat*
> *In a beautiful British Railways Passanger ferry*
> *And shouted "We're afloat, we're afloat."*
> *(To ryme with boat.)*

We hitchhike from Calais to Dunkerque youth hostel, heading on to Brussels the next day. Stephen's notebook:

When we were going there, I noticed through the trees the Atomium. It was a tremendous structure, built entirely out of steel. It looked very unearthly and Martian. We eventually got to Brussels, utterly drenched from a thunderstorm. Bridget and I went into a café, bought one cup of coffee and had half each. The waitress, witnessing our distress, refilled our small pot and gave us another cup, free. I must confess I don't think anybody in England would do that for "nasty forigners".

After Brussels we moved north along the coastline to Bergen op Zoom hostel and on to Amsterdam next day. Stephen's notebook:

We had dinner, appelsap, bread and cheese, and went to the youth hostel where we found a notice saying the hostel was fully booked for boys. So on we went to a hostel nearby called Broek en Waterland.

While we have been making our way over land and sea, our mother is preparing to fly from Newcastle. When we finally get to the airport to meet her, she is not among the passengers as we expected. Stephen's notebook:

We went to the arrivals gate, and surprise surprise, no Mum. We go to the information desk for help. Then, booming out over the loudspeakers – "Will Mrs Ashton from Newcastle please report to the airport information desk." Enter one Mum.

We went into Amsterdam by bus and then straight to the hostel where Mother soon found out what nice people the warden and his wife were. Now you may or may not know of the youth hostel rule which states that "It is necessary that each bed used is provided with one white sleeping-bag which must not be down filled." As it happened, I had omitted to bring with me a sleeping bag. I had used the blanket which I had brought in case we slept out. But as today was an occasion, I spent two shillings and hired one.

The effort of writing his notebook expires soon after this, but our mother makes a holiday scrapbook. This shows that we do indeed visit windmills and waterways and see where red cheeses are made. Broek in Waterland is only ten or so miles north of Amsterdam but it is all that we had expected the Netherlands to be. We must take a ferryboat over the harbour from the city, and then a local bus.

Wooden houses are arranged along a network of canals lined with pollarded willows and neat gardens. The local tourist service has an appealingly written brochure:

Broek in Waterland is a lovely village with about 1600 inhabitants between Amsterdam and Volendam. A few hundred years ago, very many wealthy merchants had their permanent homes in our village and many large sailing boats dropped their anchors there. Our community started to specialise in dairy-farming and now we are proud of the magnificent stock of dairy cattle. In two enterprising farms, the wife of the farmer shows you how we have made the famous Edam cheese for many centuries. You may buy, if you like, one of the cheeses. Remember there is no better tasting souvenir than such a wonderful cheese.

There is a clog-maker's shop too. Not for a minute had I really believed that people still made and wore clogs.

We travel south to Dordrecht and then north into Friesland. It often rains, but there is always a hostel drying room where we can hang up our wet clothes. Comments in our mother's scrapbook show how much she enjoys learning about the Netherlands.

A very beautiful "watery" landscape, a pretty quiet village, but the hostel unfriendly and the beds damp.

An excellent meal, a boat trip on the lake, a merry evening of games and Dutch dancing organised by the warden and his wife.

A pouring wet day, we split up on the way to Dordrecht. Bridget hitchhiked – Steve and I on the train.

Dan's mother invited us all to supper. Our first experience in a Dutch home.

Dordrecht is a beautiful and interesting town. In the afternoon we went to the museum and picture gallery.

Had a nice and spotless meal in a beautiful café.

We walked five to six miles along the sand-dunes to this very modern hostel. The only hilly landscape seen so far in Holland.

Explored the windmill, now worked by electricity. All have to revolve their sails once a month to ensure that they are safe and in working order.

A very kind man took us all around Volendam where they still wear national costume.

We had tea in this farm where Bridget and Stephen helped milk the cows and played with the little goat.

We are able to travel like this because of the system of youth hostels. The Netherlands is only a small country but it has fifty-eight hostels, all within easy reach of each other through public transport, walking or hitchhiking, as we are doing. There are rules, we know them, and we accept them. The *Nederlandse Jeugdherbergen* has a list of its rules on its booking sheet, which my mother sticks in her scrapbook.

> *1. A youth hostel is not a hotel. All guests are responsible for the cleanliness of the house and should try to leave the hostel in such a state as they wish to find the next one.*
> *2. Every guest makes up his bed and has to carry out duties as directed by the hostel father and mother.*
> *3. The use of a clean white sheet sleeping bag with attached pillow case is obligatory.*
> *4. It is not allowed to bring luggage and shoes into the dormitories.*
> *5. It is not permitted to bring intoxicants into the hostel premises.*
> *6. Smoking in the hostel is prohibited, even in the common rooms.*
> *7. The hostel is closed from 10 am until 16 pm.*
> *8. Don't rise before 7 o'clock. It is not allowed to rise earlier.*

Mary's parents, meanwhile, are visiting family friends and connections. Tonie's dictum, *it is sweet and fair to walk for the country*, truly applies here. Our mothers who have never travelled beyond the bounds of Britain have learned to love another land, and in my family's case this has been made possible by the international system of youth hostels.

5

Unknown Land

Ireland, Hereford, summer 1965

I am in Hereford's folk music club. The singer is inviting people of the road, tramps and hawker lads, to listen. I wonder if that includes girls like my friends and me. He has travelled far and wide in Scotland, and doesn't like the changes he observes, so he decides to trust in Providence and go to Ireland.

I have a new notebook because I plan to write a daily diary from now on. On the first page, I write out the words of this song.

I have not so far given much thought about visiting our neighbouring country across the sea. What do I know about Ireland? I am named Bridget after one of my mother's favourite Catholic saints. I know that I am three-eighths Irish, a quarter from my strict Irish Protestant grandmother and one-eighth from another grandparent whom I didn't know. There was a famine and the English were wicked. There was a civil war and explosions, and now Ireland is divided. That just about sums up my knowledge.

The song rings in my head. Why shouldn't I go to Ireland too? I decide to go in June. I tell my friends that, if Providence should prove true, I'll sing to them all of Erin's isle on my return. And who knows what fortune may follow from my explorations in this unknown land.

***

WESTERLY
KILKENNY, 4 JUNE 1965

I walk out of Hereford at 5.30 in the morning, heading for Fishguard, where the ferry leaves from the south of Wales for Ireland. My route first passes Hay-on-Wye and then follows the line of the Brecon Beacons as far as Llandovery. It completely avoids the industrial towns and cities of South Wales and is dreamily green and beautiful. I hear in my mind the seductive voice of the now-unfashionable Elvis Presley. I too feel wild in the country, like the deer and the dove, in the land that I love. I am heading westerly, the direction from which our winds blow wild, to Carmarthen and Haverfordwest. There I turn north towards the port of Fishguard. At one point I am near Tonie's home town of Pembroke Dock. I understand her deep sense of belonging to this lovely land.

The boat leaves at 2.30 in the afternoon, and while waiting I take a photograph of a car being swung on by a crane. Clearly that is the usual method of loading automobiles.

Once on its way, the boat sails west following the cliffs of the Welsh coastline. We pass Strumble Head lighthouse and sail towards Ireland. I am ready to explore what for me is an unknown land.

The Irish people astonish me immediately with their kindness to the stranger. My diary:

When we reached Ireland the lovely Welsh weather had turned to rainstorms. I had a few lifts to get me well away from the port, and bought some pink Irish cheese. The Irish lift-givers were truly friendly. Three sparkly-eyed women first took me to see "the narrow streets of Wexford" by which they meant the country lanes. Then two young men showed me President Kennedy's ancestral home, a tiny one-roomed hovel. They told me about leprechauns, and I saw tinker families on carts and camping in out-of-the way corners. Next, I had a lift with two middle-aged men who took me for a drink in a pub in the little town of New Ross. Here I had a pint of Beamish Stout, decidedly different from Guinness they assured me. At the pub, I learned that the Kilkenny Beer Festival was currently taking place.

I hadn't known about this, but I begin to catch the words *Fleadh Cheoil*, which I learn means a music festival, and that it is happening in a nearby town called Thurles. I find it hard to visualise the spelling, but the word *Fleadh* when spoken rhymes with *Blah*. By the time I leave the pub, darkness is falling and I need to find somewhere to pass the night. I persuade the men to leave me find a place on my own. My diary:

I was on the edge of Kilkenny, and in the first ten minutes a cottager's wife led me into a shed housing her two calves. I made a bed up with hay and my blanket, and although I was very cold I had a good night's sleep. I didn't wake until 8.30 in the morning with the noise of turkeys and calves. Mrs Meehan took me in for breakfast. She had lots of children with names like Sean, Liam, Marie, Breda and Joan. I find myself thinking that these Irish people are naturally kind but yet take no heed of their kindness. They don't fuss around as much as just take you for granted.

THE FLEADH
THURLES, 5–7 JUNE 1965

Now it is Saturday morning, and I decide to head for Thurles to discover what a *Fleadh* is all about. My map shows me that I must follow roads leading north and west. My diary:

No sooner have I left the kind Mrs Meehan when I met four Irish girls cooking breakfast by the side of the road on their Primus stove, Cora, Paula, June and Annette. "Of course we're going to Thurles. Have some porridge!" I didn't need to eat but was glad to already have made some friends. We agreed to look out for each other in Thurles. On the way out of Kilkenny there was a big cathedral, St Canice's, and I climbed to the top of the huge tower with views all around the countryside. From there, I had two lifts to Thurles, one after the other, on motor bikes, great windy open-air rides.

I have arrived at a *Fleadh*. My diary:

Crowds of people were surging around in the streets of this small town, "Tramps and Hawkers", humdingers and folksingers.

Guitars, tin whistles, bodhráns which are large round goatskin drums, harmonicas, Irish bagpipes, fiddles and even a bugle. People just sit in groups in the street playing and singing. I felt that all the folksingers from Ireland were there.

I soon meet Cora and Paula, who know lots of people here, and the day passes singing, cooking on the camp stove and of course lots of drinking Guinness all day.

They all prefer the informal music sessions in the pubs to the more formal singing and dancing competitions upon which the *Fleadh* has built its reputation. My diary:

That night, in a pub, there was singing and more singing and drinking. The Irish ballads amazed me, such a lot of them, and everyone joins in, not like England where people just don't sing. After leaving the pub, we sang in the street. June was always being asked to sing I'm a Rover, seldom sober.

A man goes up the bedroom window of his only love, in the darkness of the night. June sings this song with such tenderness that everyone focusses attention on her. His longing and her response results in gaining his love's company. It is the theme, so often in folk songs, of the wandering man pining for his love, and we empathise with his longing.

Girls like me want to be longed for too, but at the same time there is this uneasy feeling that she will be abandoned when the wanderer has gained her company. It ends predictably. Although the mountains are high above, freedom is pulling him on, leaving her to her fate. I semi-consciously absorb disquieting feelings while I accept with the others the emotion of the song.

One young man likes to sing Bob Dylan songs. But the words remind me that this handsome songster isn't looking for girls like me. Oh, no, no. If we give our hearts to a rogue, or a rover-seldom-sober, our love may be thrown back at us.

The fashion for tramps and hawkers and wild rovers is part of the youth culture here in the *Fleadh*. My new Irish friends, just like us in England, love to hitchhike through the countryside. They sing and play music in a wonderfully spontaneous and natural way. Yet these are Catholic young people, and promiscuous relationships between young men and women are still seen as immoral. I soon find out how they cope. My diary:

> *It was quite late, about 2 am when we began looking for a place to spend the night. At first, we began sleeping in a half-built house outside town. It was freezing. I shared my blanket with Cora and a boy called Neville who turned up, but naturally I froze even more with them being curled up together. So I left them, crossed the road and climbed a fifteen-foot wall to a hay barn which was full of sleeping bodies, and I rolled up in my blanket too.*
>
> *The early morning chill roused us, so we went into Thurles to look for breakfast. It was 5 am, and nothing was open. Shivering and tired, we went to Mass, because they are*

all Catholics, and there was a 6 am service. The church was full of folksingers and dossers, dragging sleeping bags and tired feet down the aisle. Cora and I slept right through Mass, slept kneeling, slept standing, slept sitting. But it was warm there.

How we longed for a cup of tea. We waited from 6.45 until 10.45 for the only café to open, but when it did the tea was delicious. The sun had meantime come out lovely and hot so off we went to sunbathe for an hour or two, camping down beside a road on the outskirts of town.

Here I decided to wash my hair. No sooner had I put it under a tap then along came two boys, one of whom was a hairdresser. "Here, let me do that!" So I had it properly washed for me. We went to their camp where they fed us chips, onion sandwiches and tea.

The group that evening who gather in another pub includes boys from Dublin who are friends of the girls, Damien, Len, Red, Paul, Leo, Gar. Damien with poetry in his speech and a sideways half smile, and Len with his enquiring gaze, are wearing natural wool-coloured Aran sweaters, hand-knitted with fishermen patterns. This is the style of these Dublin boys, a link to the countryside. Their world of music and singing and rural life is just what my Hereford friends and I love. We must surely become more closely acquainted. My diary:

These pubs all have stable yards behind, and they're great for singing. Paul was a brilliant guitarist with a voice like a corncrake. Len sang Dylan style, and everyone joined in and drank so much Guinness. Len, Cora, Red and I danced through the streets, singing Joan Baez and Dylan songs, and sang our way to the campfire where we still drank and sang. Soon I began to nod off by the fire and slept until 8 am.

This Land Is Different
Arthurstown, 8 June 1965

Now it is Monday. The long holiday weekend at the *Fleadh* is ending and all the folksingers of Ireland must make their way back to their towns for work the next day. Everyone begins packing up their camp before going into town for a last singing session in another stable yard. When Cora, June, Annette and Paula leave, we promise to write and meet again. I stay for another hour of singing with the boys. I had learned the song pronounced *Herchard of Taunton Deane* in English west country dialect from my father. My diary:

> *I sang a few Geordie songs and* Richard of Taunton Deane *in exchange for theirs, and played a few ditties squawkingly on my harmonica. Everyone is tolerant. Paul and his group of friends sang his speciality,* Alabama Baby, *adjusted for me.* Newcastle Baby, Geordie love, tell me that you love me, neath the Newcastle stars above.

There is a richness, a conviviality, which I am finding here in the *Fleadh* and have found so far everywhere in Ireland; something approachable and friendly about the people that is quite different from the staid English. I am captivated.

Leaving them, I sleep in all the lifts between Thurles and Arthurstown, where, because I've camped with my new friends at the *Fleadh*, I've saved enough money to pay the overnight fee at the youth hostel. I know certainly that I shall sing to my friends of Erin's isle when I return.

Wales Again
Pembroke Dock, 9 June 1965

After the ferry ride from Rosslare to Fishguard, I make my way to Tonie's house in Pembroke Dock so that we can return to Hereford together. Tonie's mother drops us off on the outskirts of the town to give us a start, despite her worries that we'll meet wicked men and misgivings about our habit of making friends with lorry drivers. We sing Bob Dylan songs between the lifts, and I play on my harmonica.

We stop at transport cafés for egg sandwiches and cups of tea. I am explaining to Tonie about my plan to invite my new Irish friends to hitchhike along these roads to Hereford. She is enthusiastic.

"When we leave college, let's not be teachers," she suggests. "Let's open a transport café on the A40!" I agree that it is a very good idea.

UNWILLING STUDENTS
HEREFORD, 13–17 JUNE 1965

I am not working hard. My attention is unfocused, and I seem to hope that knowledge will enter my brain with no effort on my part. I just don't seem to have the will to concentrate and begin to feel sorry for myself. My diary:

> *After a day of vagrant idling, walking through Shropshire hills, and being sleepy outside lorry depots, I had to face history swotting. I haven't learned a thing this year. Attempting to revise what hasn't been learned is ridiculous. I've been so lazy I cannot make up for it now. I'm a waster in the eyes of the world. My unhappiness is only measurable by comparison with the vastness and importance of life outside. Then it becomes as a grain of sand in the Sahara… which happy fact reminds me of our forthcoming summer holiday when Mary and I will be heading for the desert. Whether or not I return to college depends largely on my history results. If I fail hopelessly, I don't think I'll be coming back.*

Two days later, I seem to pull myself together. My diary:

> *Went straight to the library after breakfast. Learned about the First and Second World Wars. Learned kings and growth of parliaments in feudal times all afternoon and evening. Exams*

are the death of enterprise. But I've learned more history today than I learned all this year in Mr Trueman's lectures.

So that I might succour myself for this mental exertion, I need food. My diary:

Have been eating well today. Scrambled eggs at breakfast, egg custard for lunch, two nice cakes for tea, curry and ice cream for supper.

The clash between the need to study and dreams of travel drives me to write doggerel. My diary:

As I sit in my square little room
I dream of far lands and long roads,
I dream of deserts and sun and camels.
I am ready to go.
And I eat spring onions and listen to Dylan
And wait for the time to pass.
Tiny little white onions and green eating stalks,
They smell so eager to me.

During one of the boring geography lectures, Mary and I have important things to do. My diary:

We looked over our Saharan map, and planned camel routes all through Tidswell's lecture, and we talked. Thus tonight, we received a written summons from Miss Hipwell to apologise for our rudeness, which we must supply by 11 am on Monday. And this we are very reluctant to do.

As I make my way along the paths around our college, I am dreaming and singing of the desert. I have a long-playing record of the musical *The Desert Song*. On the cover is a handsome sheikh, his dark eyes gleaming under his black, winding turban as he sings to his beloved under a blue heaven where sand is kissing a moonlit sky.

The spell is thrilling. Mary and I are going to the Sahara and I shall see about handsome sheikh for myself. This English girl with her feet in the muddy fields of the Welsh borders is being pulled towards the Sahara, to the sands of Africa.

END OF TERM
HEREFORD, 18 JUNE 1965

My history exam is over, and Tonie, Jenny and Val, who are drama students, are preparing costumes for their performance of *The Beaux Stratagem*, a play by George Farquhar dating back to 1707. I stitch in two sleeves for Tonie's dress, paint a green design on Jenny's skirt and make a ruffle for Val's tri-coloured wig. Meanwhile, end-of-year tensions dominate my diary:

Sunday 20 June
Today I discovered I had a C pass for my history exam so the day's work in the library paid off. Tonie didn't do too well in her special study, and then she lost her dress for her drama display tomorrow. Jenny had two special essays to be finished by tomorrow. Carol hasn't even done hers. Mary and Chris do nothing but talk, think and practise their dance performance. Electric emotions are intense.

Tonie and I felt the need to escape. We hitched out on the Hay road. A Swiss boy gave us a lift to the Brecon Beacons. His name was Benno and he spoke very little English. He shared our picnic. We hitched back from Brecon in three potato lorries.

Tuesday 22 June
I decided to learn the guitar, and practised half a dozen chords which I strum in a tinny way. I had to run away from Matron who caught me playing on my harmonica again. I wish we didn't have to waste these two weeks. Summer is here. The weather is tantalising, the political situation in Algeria is disturbing. The clock in Hereford is just striking midnight. The night is so still that the sound carries easily.

Thursday 24 June 1965
Horrible Tidswell summoned Mary and me in for a gruesome interview about our rudeness of last Friday. He's waiting for an apology. We mumbled something or other, and escaped.

BETTER THAN A LECTURE
HEREFORD, 29 JUNE 1965

"I just don't feel like sitting in the geography lecture," says Tonie early in the morning. "Let's go somewhere interesting."

I don't take much tempting. "How about Anglesey? Could we do it in a day, there and back?"

It is 8.15 am, and we walk out of Hereford along the road northward.

An agricultural vehicle passes us by and stops. Something is bellowing and stamping in the trailer behind.

"I can take you to Oswestry," says the cheerful driver. "That is, if you don't mind the company of a bull in the back."

We clamber into the cab. He isn't asking us to share the trailer, fortunately. "It is a Hereford bull worth £2000," he tells us. "I'm delivering him to Lord Middleton's castle."

When he drops us off, we join the old coaching route of the A5 with its milestones and are soon in a bakery wagon delivering bread into Wales. Once past Betws y Coed, our driver stops to let us take a photo of a stone and wooden cottage called the Ugly House. The day is hot and the North Wales scenery enticing. Beyond Capel Curig, we reach Llyn Ogwen, a lake left behind by the melting glaciers of the last Ice Age. We are so hot we ask our driver to let us out and, removing our outer layer of clothes, we leap into the ice-cold water. The Snowdon range is visible through the heat haze. We can see the striking peaks of Tryfan and the Glyder to our left, mountains that have been shaped by ice movements. Tonie writes in her notebook:

> *It was awkward getting a lift down this terribly twisty Nant Ffrancon Pass, but at last came a wagon which was going to the new power station on Anglesey. We went through the immense slate quarries of Bethesda where the walling is all done with slabs of slate.*
>
> *The wagon driver drops us off on the outskirts of Bangor, and suddenly we are at the Menai Bridge, which connects the Welsh mainland to the island of Anglesey. It is white and graceful against the blue of the sky, and we walk over it feeling hypnotised as we look down to the sea below.*
>
> *Hungry as ever, we find a tearoom in Anglesey where we spend an extravagant amount of money on eggs, bread and butter and tea. We know if we are to make our way back to Hereford before the inflexible curfew time of 10.30 we had better turn around.*

"Where you heading, young ladies?" calls out a man who is painting the bridge. Tonie's notebook:

> *Met a Bridge Goblin who begins at the start of each year to paint the whole bridge. At the end of the year, when he has finished, it is time to start all over again. He lives in a little wooden cradle which hangs over the side of the bridge, and*

dangles above the calm waters of the straits. Ideal place for suicides!

When we tell him we must be back in Hereford by 10.30, he grins. "You might be lucky."

Three lifts take us back to Shrewsbury, the last one in the open air on the back of a lorry. The wind is blowing exhilaratingly through our hair. We make good time arriving at Ludlow, only twenty miles from Hereford, a town with attractive black and white half-timbered houses. Here, happy, tidy people are heading to see a festival production of *Hamlet* in the castle. We feel untidy and unsuitable. We leave, and are soon picked up by a man in a little blue sports car. He kindly drives us right up to the college entrance, enabling us to arrive by 9.30 pm. The 300-mile round trip has been achieved comfortably. We've crossed the rolling border hills into Wales, observed the glaciated scenery of Snowdonia with its lakes, crossed the bridge over the Menai Straits briefly into Anglesey, and walked among the vernacular architecture of Ludlow. We've learned quite a lot of geography.

"You were lucky you missed Tidswell's lecture," Mary tells us, serving tea as we collapse onto the bed in her room. "It was so boring. He was going on about isobars, and I don't remember a thing."

TIME TO MOVE
HEREFORD, 30 JUNE 1965

Our final results come in and somehow we have all passed. Tonie, Jenny and I have managed C average. Val has done better with a B credit, and Mary has an A distinction for her dance course. No-one has failed or ended with a D despite our fears and woes. Gradually people are packing and leaving. Mary and I have our second smallpox jabs and five minutes later we crash our bikes into each other in Broad Street. I lie sprawled across the street while a lorry screeches to a halt a foot away from me. I wonder if I'll leave England alive, never mind get to the desert. Tonie is feeling depressed because she has found that she must go into town lodgings for the next academic year as there is a shortage of rooms in the student hostels. Ivor rings up, and she weepingly tells him the bad news. He says comfortingly, "It doesn't matter, luv."

SNAKES IN AFRICA
SWINDON, 1–5 JULY 1965

Mary and I start on our long journey. We hitchhike to Swindon, and we are given a lift by an engineer from Birmingham. He had spent seven years in North Africa. My diary:

He told us all about black lace snakes, six-inch scorpions, lizards, white slave traders, rampant disease, cruel marriage customs, venereal disease, the killing heat, and more. But he didn't put us off at all.

We feel invulnerable. We are heading for the Sahara.

6

Long Hot Roads South

France, Italy, Sicily, summer 1965

"Bridget, don't you realise there has been a military coup in Algeria?" my father tells me when I ring him at our house in Newcastle. My sister Rosie has told me that he is worrying. "There is unrest, and you could be in danger."

"Don't worry, Dad," I say. "We'll be careful. Who would want to harm us?" I really have no idea if this is true or not. The phone in the public call box beeps – and cuts me off.

It is harder still to reassure my frantic mother. "Darling, you don't know the way. You don't speak the language. How will you eat? Where will you sleep?" All the things mothers usually worry about.

"Rosie is coming with us through France," I tell her. My young sister will see us on our way. We must do our geography field work in Brittany and the Massif Central before moving on to Italy and over the Mediterranean. My mother is not reassured, but nothing will stop us. We will go to Africa. Optimism is in our bones.

***

THE BARNS OF FRANCE
ALONG THE WAY, 6–8 JULY 1965

Rosie, Mary and I are in a lorry that is driving through London. My diary:

> *Our lorry drivers gave us coffee and cigarettes. It was fun riding through London seeing Hyde Park speakers, demonstrations at Trafalgar Square, the Tower, St Paul's Cathedral, Tower Bridge. We sat on the back of the lorry as we went through Bermondsey. The drivers set us off onto the A2, on our way to Dover, from where we caught the 10.30 pm boat to Calais. Farewell to England, to the white cliffs and coloured lights in the darkness. We shrieked with excitement as we left on our grands vacances.*

Hitching from Calais to Brittany takes a couple of days, and we meet characters good and bad along the way. "*Donnez-moi une petite caresse*," says a driver, who had lied and told us he was going to Rouen, in our direction, but in fact was heading for Paris. We escape from his car, which he has parked in the woods, and leave him. Our next lift is with a charming Frenchman who gives us fruit and buys us coffee. At night, we stop at a village and an old lady wearing sabots takes us to a farm, where we sleep warm and cosy in a barn of fresh hay. The family gives us a good breakfast of oranges, tomatoes, bread and coffee. Our first lift next day is with a Belgian man whose lunchtime stop is at a transport café, where he buys Mary and Rosie some cold meat, and me some Camembert cheese, all with crispy bread and butter. Our next lift is with two weedy Frenchmen who immediately drive us off the main road and demand, "*Voulez-vous faire le bel amour?*"

I am angry. Mary laughs, and Rosie doesn't say a word. Not exactly sure where we are, we leave them near some forests and a chateau, and begin to trek back towards the main road. A kindly young man then takes us well into the Breton countryside of woods and small fields, where horses are pulling loaded haycarts. We are near our destination when we come across a man exhibiting himself. We walk past him uncertainly without looking backwards. Although we are only about twenty kilometres from Saint-Gilles-Pligeaux, our destination, it is about 9.30 pm and no more cars are passing. We sit on a crossroads and sing, waiting, hoping, chatting to the occasional people who pass by. In the end, feeling we can get no further, we approach a farmer. He is much amused at these three English girls who have rolled up unannounced asking to sleep in his barn, but he obliges. We have our supper of bread and coffee, and once again curl up in sweet-smelling hay. The dog senses our presence and barks for what seems hours. We fear the rearrival of the exhibitionist man, especially when Mary sits up and says, "I'm not quite sure if I can see some eyes…"

To Milk The Cows
Saint-Gilles-Pligeaux, 8–12 July 1965

I've always wanted to improve my skill at the hand-milking of cows and at the Berthelot farm I have my chance. We have arrived at the farm where the family and I had become acquainted last summer, and Saint-Gilles-Pligeaux is the village I have chosen for my geography special study. The family happily allows us to make ourselves comfortable in their barn. In between milking sessions, I go to the *mairie*, the town hall, where I am permitted to trace maps to show land-use transects of the village and copy plans of the chateau's territory. Mary and Rosie accompany me over the next few days as I draw maps of village building use, discovering that each little stone-built house has a granary upstairs. We follow old routeways, and find granite tors, prehistoric monuments and ancient field systems. This is the kind of geography that I love. And each morning and evening I get a little better at milking the cows, even though I only manage one and a half cows compared to

Claudine Berthelot's five and a half. Perhaps it would be better said that she finished my second one for me.

At another farm we have made a friend called Daniel, who invites us to his house where his mother is making crêpes. Mixing the flour with eggs, she spreads the mixture on a round flat gas-heated plate, and then lets Mary and me make our own, which we wash down with plenty of cider. In the evening, Monsieur Berthelot translates lots of Breton place names for me into French and answers all my questions about his farm. All the young people have gone dancing, but Mary, Rosie and I can't go with them as we have neither suitable clothes nor entrance fee. We do however manage to come up with sixty centimes each to clean ourselves at the *douches municipales*, the town showers, where we remove our clothes for the first time in a week.

We are so dirty and it takes us so long that by the time we have finished there is a great queue of people waiting to get in.

Return to Chambon
Parthenay, 13 July 1965

It is time for us to hitchhike off towards the Vallée de Chaudefour to attend to Mary's field work. The first evening, we stop at the village of Parthenay. We are not alone. Other young people, like us, are hitching along all the roads of France in this lovely summer weather, going wherever they have chosen. We knock on a farmhouse door. My diary:

The woman was in bed. She answered that she had no straw or barn but she gave us a mattress and blankets to take to the granary. The night is warm and still. Below our shuttered windows are tree-lined streets where other hitch-hikers are moving along. A big moon is rising, with a red sunset sky in the other direction. Crickets are yikkering and we have the whole sense of being in France. It is so warm that we can sleep without clothes, as in Spain. So unlike England.

Two Shillings A Day
Chambon, 14 July 1965

La Mère Aubergiste, the hostel mother, at Chambon is pleased to see us again, remembering our two previous visits in 1964. This will be our base for a few days, partly staying in the hostel but saving money by sleeping in the barn over the road at night. We are living on two shillings a day, which doesn't cover both food and overnight fee. Choices must be made.

As in Saint-Gilles-Pligeaux, the *mairie* officials are very helpful and supply Mary with the maps she needs. Over the next few days, often in the pouring rain, we study the church architecture and village settlement patterns. We make our way to the hamlet of Bresouléille, high on the plateau, where the farmhouses have barns above the living quarters and are cut into the steep hillside. Along the way, we find and eat lots of wild strawberries. But we also manage to get lost while doing our land-use survey, and scramble through prickles, thorns, slugs, grasshoppers and gorse, over rocks, down sandy slippery slopes, all barefoot because our broken shoes won't stay on.

Managing To Eat
Chambon, 15–16 July 1965

Despite all the hazards, Mary is making progress with her work. And we are sticking to our minimal budget. My diary:

Had a good-morning awakening in our barn from a moustached old farmer in a black Auvergne hat. We crept into the hostel and stole enough bread ends to make a breakfast of dry fried bread and coffee. We're living on two shillings a day and we hardly eat anything except bread dipped in black coffee, sometimes fried if we can steal any fat. At lunchtime in Chambon, we used our daily allowance to buy delicious St Nectaire cheese, lettuce and eggs.

Danny and Serge are the two boys Mary and I had met in Murol the year before. We head for the *grande danse* as today is a national holiday. My diary:

The people at the dance were town types. But there was Danny Papon with his wife! What a surprise! She was gorgeous and friendly. Serge is in the militaire. Mary and Rosie were enjoying the dance, but I sat on the steps where boys came pestering. We left in the rain and hitched back in one lift to the lovely warm barn, with soft hay and millions of bugs.

We have made friends with a boy called Bernard who will accompany Rosie on her hitchhiking journey back to Paris. She leaves with our maps and plans, taking them to England for us, and Mary and I are off, finally, to the Sahara. My diary:

We washed, packed and paid La Mère Aubergiste at the hostel, so we only have one centime left. We owe the farmer's wife 33 cents. But we found some bottles, cashed them in Chambon, were able to pay our debts and buy some bread for lunch. We have done the last two weeks on £2.

Peach Farm
Pizançon, 17 July 1965

Mary and I are now in a peach farm in France, on one side of the Alps. Italy is on the other side. Only this morning we'd been in the

Massif Central eating St Nectaire cheese. We'd travelled through the Cévennes with a Monte-Carlo style driver, who had driven on two wheels round the bends, to Valence. My diary:

> *We were starving hungry and shaky, so we sat down promptly in the nearest sunny spot in the main street and ate bread and half a tomato each. A boy came along who said he had no more money than us, but he gave us his last 30 cents as he can get some more tomorrow, he said. Then we had 31 cents, but we couldn't buy anything with that. We found a potato as we hitched out of Valence. That'll do for tomorrow.*
>
> *Our first lift from Valence has taken us to this peach farm, and we are writing our diaries in the shed surrounded by the most tantalising fruity smells. My diary:*
>
> *But we aren't stealing any peaches because the people here are being so kind to us. There are two children, aged twelve and ten years, who speak a little English, and are very charming and curious with us.*
>
> *What I like is the contrast of this hitchhiking life. This morning we were watching farmers' hands pressing St Nectaire cheese on an Auvergne farm. Tonight we're on a genuine peach farm at the foot of the Alps. Crickets are yikkering outside, and tomorrow we'll be crossing the Alps.*

Over The Alps
Farm of midges, 18 July 1965

Our honesty is rewarded. My diary:

> *The farmer this morning gave us a great bag of peaches of which we've eaten half already. We have no money at all, five peaches to half a loaf of bread for breakfast. We're planning on not getting any money out at all in Italy, seeing how easy*

it will be to do without. With the money we save I'll buy some material and make a new skirt. My old one is slowly dropping to bits.

We easily get lifts towards the Alps. I habitually write a diary, but now Mary has decided to write one too:

After Grenoble, slowly we begin our ascent of the Alps. It is so beautiful we cannot think of enough words to describe what we feel. A woman gives us a lift up the valley of the Romanche to the Col of Lautaret. The ascent is steeper now and the mountains all around are enormous, the highest ones covered in snow. The River Romanche began as snow meltwater. The woman stops to let us take a photograph on the watershed, surrounded by mountains. We can hardly believe we were crossing the Alps, on top of the world surrounded by blue skies, sunshine and mountains.

At the Italian border, Mary's notebook records our financial plans:

Bridge changed some money, ten shillings only for films and postcards. We don't plan to use any money as we go through Italy. We have £25 to see us all the way across to the desert and to get us back to England.

Our passports are stamped, and suddenly we are in Italy. We pass down through white limestone valleys with villages on the most unlikely rock perches. In Turin, we are dropped off on the outskirts of the city, where we compare the dark-haired young people with those of Spain. The girls look more modern but the boys are much the same. One little white car after another pulls up along the road. "*Ciao, signorine inglesi. Vieni con me!*" Hello, English girls. Come with me! They are mostly young and good-looking but the pressure is intense. We can hardly think what to do. Every few steps we take, a car stops, and we say "*No, no, signor*", trying to walk quickly on. We are hot and tired, and our bags feel heavy. In the end, we accept a lift from a young man who seems to understand our predicament. He takes us to a farm in the countryside in the direction we need to go. My diary:

> It was difficult to explain to the farmer what we wanted, but he offered us his barn and invited us to eat which was welcome because we had only eaten a few peaches and a meagre slice of bread at the peach farm this morning. He gave us lovely tomatoes, sticks of bread and a most delicious Italian cheese with black rind. We slept in the open-air barn, with only our blankets and no sweater as it was so warm. But there were millions of biting midges and flies everywhere.

I pay the penalty. The midges obviously prefer me to Mary. I have been bitten all over my arms, feet and the one uncovered side of my face. My skin burns agonisingly all next day without respite.

ITALIAN AUTOSTRADE
ITALIAN LORRY, 19 JULY 1965

Our lifts follow the rivers that drain into the Po on the Plain of Lombardy. My diary:

> We approach the Tuscan Hills where Michelangelo worked in the quarries for stone to cut his marbles. I am hoping to stop in Florence for a day or two. The two Italians who give us a lift can't keep their hands on the driving wheel. Hence we can hardly concentrate on the tree-covered mountain scenery. STOP INTERDIT signs are plentiful along the motorway, but we make such a fuss that the men angrily stop to let us out in the middle of nowhere, traffic rushing past.

This is Italy, and rules are made to be broken. A huge lorry transporting Fiat cars stops. The two drivers are polite. "*Andiamo a Napoli*," they tell us. We are going to Naples. Plans to stop in Florence and Rome must be forgotten if we accept the ride. Deciding to trust them, we make a hasty decision while the traffic on the road thunders past. We clamber up into the cab, which is big enough to have a curtained sleeping compartment behind the seats.

At nine in the evening, the lorry drivers stop for a meal at a *trattoria*. All we've had this day was the cheese and bread at the farm. We are really hungry and have been drinking water to assuage the pangs. This is our first Italian meal. Mary's notebook:

> *First we are presented with some fantastic spaghetti which we wash down with wine. Next comes a real beef steak – marvellous but not for Bridget who was given cheese – with a peculiar purple pepper thing, not quite so nice. Then a whole bowl of fruit in water is placed on the table. The meal is finished off with coffee and anisette. To thank them, we play them a tune or two and dance about. When they were satisfied that we couldn't play very well, we left in the lorry. I had a good sleep on the top bunk. The drivers limited themselves to gentle hair pulling, but we managed to sleep.*

We travel all through the night, my midge bites burning painfully. As daylight comes, we watch a red sunrise over cliffs and sea. Slowly we are approaching Naples. Donkey carts with farmers going to work are passing along the roads.

By 5.30 am we have arrived. The drivers pose for us to take a photo of them and their lorry. It has been good to travel with kind, courteous Italian lorry drivers. Before they leave, they point to the skyline.

Volcanic
Naples, 20–21 July 1965

A volcano? We are looking at Vesuvius. Somehow it hadn't occurred to us that we'd actually see a volcano.

Our packs are heavy and we need to pause. We decide to go down to the sea and rest before catching the evening boat to Tunis. At least, that is our roughly formulated plan, but this is a Latin country. There is no peace at all for two unaccompanied Northern European girls. As we walk down the hill, young men pester us endlessly. Finally, we give in to the persuasions of two handsome young men. We simply don't have enough resistance.

They take us to the beach. Angelo slips off for a moment and returns with two single red roses. Clearly there is a further motive. However, Antonio and Toni are charming company, and we simply respond to their enthusiasm. We are hungry as usual, and glad when they take us to eat. We have pizza. I have never heard of such a dish. It is a Neapolitan speciality, they tell us, a rounded base of freshly baked bread with tomato sauce with anchovies and a sprinkling of cheese on top: poor people's cheap food. In my diary I call the cheese "Marselli or something".

We are getting to know these boys. Angelo is dark and Italian-looking, with black lustrous hair and smiling eyes. Toni by contrast tells us his father is German, and he is fair, with blue eyes. His eyes are smiling too. When the boys realise that we are geography students and like rocks, they put us in their car and drive us to Vesuvius. Can this be true? Are we really going to visit a volcano? Mary's notebook:

> The narrow road is cut into the outflow of lava from the volcano, with fantastic rock shapes. We look back to Naples. It is a blazing hot day and a blue haze covers the city. It is impossible to explain how happy we are. Angelo takes the car to the bottom of the chair lift. Now we are going the rest of the way up Vesuvius. As the chairlift leaves the station, a sort of peace transcends. All that can be heard is the smooth rolling of the wheels on the wire. The higher we go, the more fantastic the view. Angelo is gorgeous. We arrive at the top and then walk up on volcanic material to the crater. It is massive. The rocks are in layers of eruptions and vary in red tones of colour. At one or two places steam forces its way to the surface. We still can't really believe that we are on top of Vesuvius, something we saw amidst dusty clouds this morning, never dreaming we would go up it. We came back down on the chair lift, through the same peaceful atmosphere. Would you like to visit the garden with the fountain, the boys ask us next.

The path in the garden wanders into silent woodlands, where the boys try a little *amore*. Although we like them, this is much too fast. Toni and I are communicating as well as we can in French and he is just about manageable, but I frequently hear Mary's cries of indignation. But we decide to accept their invitation to stay one day longer in Naples because we are invited to Angelo's house to meet his family. This seems to hold some prospect of respectability. My diary:

> *Immediately the family sits us down to eat. These Italians eat so much in a three-course meal! I am bursting after an enormous dish of macaroni, never mind facing eggs, oily vegetables, cheese and fruit, all with plentiful bread and wine. And after the meal, off we go to visit Naples by night. "I love my Napoli," says Angelo.*

The fun is about to begin. The boys drive us out of Naples to a little promontory called Capo Miseno, twenty kilometres from the city. In the romantic darkness of the Neapolitan night, stars are twinkling and the lighthouse is beaming. My diary:

> *Toni, with his Germanic origin, was not so frantic as Angelo. Poor Mary yelled for me every few minutes. We were on our blankets on the beach. I've never seen Mary quite so furious with a man before. He had broken numerous promises. I was cross too, and tempers were beginning to fray. "Perché non fare l'amore?" It sounded like French. Why not make love? I did my best in mixed French and English. But when you can't explain "why" in a foreign language, friction springs easily. Mary walked off in an upset rage, and it took Angelo a while to realise she really meant No.*
>
> *The row between Toni and me came later. He lost his temper, and as I can't lose my temper in French I could only swear back in English. However, as we were a long way from Naples, and half our baggage was at Angelo's house, we had to be diplomatic.*

Mary's notebook makes it clear that Angelo had broken his promises to respect her wishes. But she had been so firm, so angry, that in the end he was upset to think that she found him bad and dishonest. My diary:

> In the morning everything was very delicate. But since they had realised that we meant what we said, you couldn't want two more agreeable chaps. Gradually we all forgave each other and went for a swim in the cool blue morning sea.
> Later, they took us to a remote cliff top where we lay in the shade looking down over the idyllic scene of blue sea and boats and islands and tufa cliffs with two most gorgeous men who behaved beautifully all afternoon. After a last huge meal at Angelo's house, they took us to the port for the boat to Sicily. They were charming about last night, and as we prepare to part, Toni gave me a souvenir which really touched me. It was his medal for winning a parachute-jumping competition. And he gave me his philosophy of life – to learn and study all there is to know about everything, but first and foremost, l'amore.

I smile, but I think to myself that this is all very well for a single young man who is not left with the consequences of importunate love.

At the gate to the port, the officials stop the boys from coming through to see us off. Mary's notebook:

> Toni has a chat with them and tells them we are their fairies and they won't see us for a long time. He wins and they are allowed through. It's awful knowing that soon we will leave these two Italians behind us, a mere incident in our time in Napoli. They had not been able to understand us at all. We promise to write – we feel so sad. As we go aboard, already we are being pestered by others. Still, if these two had not pestered us we'd never have come to know them. The hooter blows, the gangway is pulled down, and the ship slowly moves away from the quay. We see Toni's white shirt fading in the distance.

It's sad having to leave people especially when you have just managed to create an understanding of sorts in mixed Italian and English. Angelo and Toni really made our stay here.

Unlike as in many songs, this time the female wanderers are leaving the boys behind. Our ship sails out into the darkness towards Sicily; we wave to Toni and Angelo and watch the lights of Naples slowly disappear.

Two More Boys
Palermo, 22 July 1965

The clifftops of Sicily are appearing as we wake with the sunrise. We have spent our moonlight Mediterranean cruise sleeping on the deck in the soft warm night air. Perhaps we'll be a little less vulnerable to masculine enthusiasm in Sicily. I have a penfriend in Palermo. I'd met Franco Vaccaro in Paris a year or so ago, and we've corresponded regularly. We plan to visit his family. My diary:

The bay of Palermo crowds the city in between great cliffs of white, yellow and gold rocks. As we were walking off the

> *boat, into those baking hot tree-lined streets, we were tired but so excited, bearing the heat like an extra load on our backs. We were hungry too, so we ate a little of our cheese and bread supplies in the streets. And sure enough, along come two handsome Sicilian boys. Although we mean to resist, somehow we don't. Their names are Mario and Marco. They drive us off to swim at a beach, in the silver cool water, with the sun really blazing hot. Despite us feeling strange about more boyfriends after Toni and Angelo, we like these boys. But we told them from the start: "Non fare l'amore!"*

Agreeably, they drive us to Franco's family house, and as the family is at home they leave us there, arranging to call again in the evening. My diary:

> *Franco has gone off to Rome four days ago. He is a soldier in the militare. His grandmother, mother, father and little sister Patricia were all here. They gave us a fantastic welcome and we could speak a little French to his father so it wasn't dead end conversation. They gave us eggs, cheese, pears and coffee, and we were very very hungry.*

We leave a note on the door for Marco and Mario to say that we are going out with the family in the evening. They drive us along cliff roads and beside beaches, and then treat us to strawberry ice cream. Back home we have what we are learning is the typical huge Italian meal: spaghetti, cheese or meat, salad, fruit, all with wine and bread, and coffee to finish. I just can't manage it all. For the first time in a while, we are sleeping on a bed. The air is so warm that we need no bedclothes at all.

Treasures Of The City
Palermo, 23 July 1965

"*Buongiorno*," says Signor Vaccaro as he shakes Mario's hand next day. He speaks emphatically to the boys, and we understand the gist of what he is saying. "Bridget is Franco's friend. You must be respectful to her and Mary." Thank goodness for that.

"*Camminiamo un po*," suggests Signor Vaccaro. We can guess what he means. Let's walk a little. Along the pathways of the parks, lined with palm trees, we take the Sicilian air. Marco and Mario walk politely with Mary and me, no handholding or touching, and Franco's parents with little Patricia follow a few metres behind. There will be no funny business, and we have relief from Italian *amore*.

During the rest of the day, after leaving the Vaccaro family, the boys proudly show us some of the treasures of Palermo, beautiful churches with golden interiors, one with Arabic domes, others with cloisters. The quiet gardens are filled with orange trees, lemons, cactus with wooden stems and fruit, papyrus and scented jasmine. This is paradise. And when we are tired they take us to a lonely beach to rest and swim. There is a limit to the self-discipline of these boys, and we are obliged to remind them with "*Non fare l'amore*, remember?" until they return us to Franco's house.

The family are packing up to go on holiday. "Goodbye, goodbye. *Arrivederci.* Come again when Franco is at home." After warm embraces, we go our separate ways.

The boat for Tunis doesn't leave until Tuesday, and this is Saturday, so Mary and I have decided we will explore the island.

"But you can't go off around Sicily all alone," Mario and Marco insist. "It is dangerous. The *Mafia* kill people, murder people. They are everywhere, and they are in control." We believe them, but we don't see why anyone would want to murder us. We decide to take no notice. We'll have a three-day tour of the island. We have little or no Italian money but the nights are warm and we have blankets. We know from experience that people are likely to feed us. There's nothing to worry about except unwanted *amore*. My diary:

> Mario and Marco drove us off to camp out somewhere for the night. They were highly perplexed at us sleeping out, and full of the dangers of the wild, dry Sicilian hinterland. However, they took us to an olive grove and here we prepared our blankets. To our great surprise, they just gave a quick goodnight peck and left us in peace. We slept like logs.

Poverty And Riches
Farm near Etna, 24 July 1965

Mary and I have grown up in the green fields and sooty towns of England and Wales, where rain is frequent, the winds are always cool, and rivers flow all year round. The Mediterranean lands are a source of wonder to us. My diary over the next few days is filled with landscape descriptions as we roam across the island. We know this is a poor country, a land of emigrants who leave in search of a better life. Yet the climate, the plants, the agriculture and the glorious historic buildings in Palermo are of a richness that enchants us. My diary:

We left our olive grove at eight in the morning and headed into the heart of upland Sicily. It is all huge pointed dry mountains with cultivation in the most unlikely and unrewarding places, herds of sheep and goats, and bony cows here and there guarded by single herdsmen. The heat was blazing, the wind was strong and hot. We saw fantastic examples of water erosion. It must be flood erosion, we thought, as it hardly ever rains here. There were miniature Grand Canyons, great empty gullies working their way down from mountains. Almost all the rivers were dry, though one or two trickled muddily along. Villages were perched on pinnacles of rocks. Our lift man took us to Enna, an acropolis town. He fed us with peaches, grapes and cheese sandwiches at the foot of the castle walls of Enna.

"Are you English? German?" A girl approaches us. She tells us that she is German. She has married a Sicilian boy and lives in this idyllic hilltop town. Could we be so enraptured with a handsome Italian boy that we might do the same? In this sunny weather of long languorous days of freedom, anything feels possible.

Having had our first experience of a volcano in Naples, now we are close to Etna. Our lift takes us as far as the village of Paternò in a land of orange groves. The view of Etna dominates the skyline. As soon as we get out of the car, boys arrive from all sides. Trying to get rid of them, and needing somewhere to stay for the night, we eventually appeal for sanctuary at a farm. We are welcomed with open arms by a large family of men, women and children. They give us the usual enormous meal. My diary:

As evening arrives, and I am ready to end my day, they take us off to dance and drink at the house of some relations. I am so tired I want to sleep. But as no-one sleeps here until 2 am or so, I had to try to stay awake. Mary was loving it, and dancing merrily. An overweight, pot-bellied man insisted on dancing with me all the time, and everyone thought it a huge joke. Eventually we were allowed to sleep on a big soft comfortable bed and knew nothing until the morning.

We are having a cross-cultural experience. On one hand, we are truly thankful to have been given food and hospitality by this family, and yet we find them overwhelming. Because they know we want to go to Etna, it is hard to resist their enthusiasm when they insist on taking us. We'd prefer to go quietly on our own, but we accept politely. My diary:

The mountain was beautiful, lots of small volcanos sprouting up all along the slopes, and black and red lava everywhere. The volcano was smoking more today than yesterday. We didn't go up in the funicolare as it was too expensive for our hosts. However, they took us for a close look at one of the small side craters, burnt out, with a hole which seemed to go down to the bottom of the earth. Yes, the mountain was beautiful. But the men were blessed menaces. All their wives and girlfriends were around, and yet they still pestered. Mary always has a good sense of humour and thought it was a joke, but it got on my nerves. I don't know how the women put up with it all the time.

My diary continues with comments which are not particularly polite. I write that the main difference between these country people and us is their lack of education. They are certainly kind and generous. The educated Italian people we have spent time with so far, like Toni and Angelo, Mario and Marco, and Franco's family, are very different. Needing to get away from the clamour and the incessant talking, we leave them fortunately with goodwill on both sides and hitch south towards Catania.

Three In A Bed
Ragusa, 25 July 1965

In our next lift, we are serenaded by a young Sicilian man. Squashed in the back of the car between us, his powerful love songs fill the air, while the dark-haired gypsy-like man in front handles the steering wheel as if it were the reins of a swift horse. His girlfriend, seated beside him, gets thrown around laughing. The sun is setting making dark shadows of the mountains as we tear round horseshoe bends, passing towns deep in gorges or perched on cliffs. We are dropped off by the roadside into another warm night and begin to wonder where we'll sleep. Another man stops.

"*No, signorine, non è sicuro,*" he insists. It is not safe to sleep in the fields. We are finding that Sicilian people are always concerned for our welfare. It is all rather different from the terrifying *Mafia* that Marco and Mario had warned us about. My diary:

> *Eventually, after the usual unsuccessful persuasion to lure us into amore, he took us to his house where we met his wife and bambinos. We were given the typical enormous meal, which in my case included lots of beer and cheese.*
>
> *"You sleep here with me." His wife shows us a huge bed. So Mary and I lie down with her and the three of us sleep like logs.*

Temple Of Juno
Palermo, 26 July 1965

Next day we pass through lands more fertile than the mountainous regions we've crossed. Here is more cultivation, almond trees, tomatoes and vines. Herdsmen are leading goats with long, beautiful horns to water. We walk a little and ride a little. Hitchhiking is never a problem. One man giving us a ride stops the car on a lonely hillside. He gestures us to leave the car.

We get out and realise that we are looking at a Greek temple, standing strong against the skyline. He tells us in Italian that this is the temple of Juno, and the words are similar enough to be comprehensible.

The temple is just standing there. No signs. No fences, tourist cabins, car parks, caféterias or evidence of heritage industry. It is a simple Greek temple made of golden stone on a hill.

This is where the ancient Greeks worshipped the queen of heaven. Men and women in white gowns were here, looking down over the sea and the mountains, as we are now. On this day, 26 July 1965, no-one else is there. This is our moment.

Back in the car, I am so drowsy with the heat that I drop off to sleep, and Mary tells me later about the other temples she saw through car window as the car drove along.

Our driver drops us off at an upland crossroads, and now we truly learn what it means to be hot. There is no shade, no relief. The maize is ripening in the fields below, and the whole landscape of hill and plain is being baked as if in an oven. Stirling Moss, or his double, saves us from this relentless exposure by stopping to offer us a lift. He drives at an average of sixty miles per hour around precipitous mountain roads and puts us down in Palermo at five o'clock.

"Hello, Maria; hello, Bridget." We have contacted Marco in a public telephone box. "You are OK? We'll come in a moment." They take us for a cooling swim at Mondello beach.

"No *Mafia*," we assure them. "We were always safe. Sicilian people are kind." We are glad to relax in the familiarity of their friendship. We visit Marco's house, though clearly his mother is a little uncertain about the nature of our relationship with her son. That night, the boys take us to a beach hut belonging to his family, where they leave us in peace. No matter that the wooden floor is hard, we are so tired that it feels like a bed of rose petals, and no Italian voices are exhausting us.

Unclaimed Hearts
Ferryboat, 27 July 1965

At five o'clock in the morning, the noise starts. Boom, boom, boom on the wooden walls of the cabin. We lie quietly, pretending we are not here, and eventually whoever it is goes away. A little later, the booming starts again. By this time, we are dressed and we peep through the slats, hoping that we can't be seen. A woman is there with a little girl and we catch the word *carabinieri*, policeman. What would the police do if they find us here? We won't take the chance of finding out. When the woman and child go off, we slip out of the hut and go to swim in the sea before telephoning the boys again.

Mario and Marco are kind to us. Franco's father has probably had the right effect. They take us to the hillside chapel of Santa Rosalia, Palermo's saint, who looks down over the valley of fruit trees towards the sea. And we have more enormous meals. But it is time to go. We have reached the southern tip of Europe, wildly exotic and beautiful, with its dark-haired, lustful men, people who always want to feed us, dry arid landscapes, and a Greek temple lonely on a hillside. We've made friends with handsome boys but haven't fallen in love. Our hearts are still unclaimed. My diary:

The boys took us to the boat. There was the usual fuss getting tickets and showing passports. Once on board, we waved goodbye to them. The boat left the city surrounded by its cliffs as the sun was going down, the inky-blue sea swishing by. We followed the coastline of Sicily for several hours, well into darkness, watching the lights of the towns shining out from the land.

Our nights have been spent in a midge-infested barn, on the rear cabin of a transport lorry, on a clifftop near Naples, under olive trees and in a seaside cabin in Sicily. Now we shall sleep on the deck. There we lie, under the stars, our blankets wrapped around us as the evening air cools down. We are between one continent and another, between the Europe that we know, just a little, and Africa, which we know not at all.

7

Call Of The Desert

North Africa, Spain, summer 1965

We walk down the streets of Tunis, gazing at our surroundings, two girls from the rural green world of England and the Welsh borders – and we are speechless. We know, or we should know, what to expect in a Muslim country, yet the reality of it all astonishes us.

We are shy about seeming to stare. "The women look like nuns," we whisper to each other. In their white robes, with just their eyes showing, they look dignified and modest. The men wear red fezzes and flowing gowns, or just old robes and sloppy sandals.

Legs are nowhere to be seen. We feel self-conscious in our knee-length skirts, but because we are walking with an English boy from Bristol whom we'd met on the boat we are avoided by passing men, who must assume that we are spoken for.

***

With A Map
Tunis, 28 July 1965

We head to the British consulate to tell the people there where we are going in case we become lost in an unknown wilderness. We are heading for the desert, and our parents certainly don't know where we are.

"Are you sure you know what you're doing?" the young man behind the desk enquires. "You haven't got any definite address for me to note down. And did you realise that there has just been a military coup in Algeria, that the president, Ahmed Ben Bella, has been deposed and has disappeared? That there is a new president, Houari Boumédiène?"

We have vaguely heard this, but our plans won't change.

"We are going to the desert," we tell him. "We will be returning through Spain, so we need to travel across Algeria to get to Morocco. And then we will go over the Atlas Mountains to the Sahara."

"How will you find your way?" he asks.

"We have a map," we reply, and show him our cheap road map.

The clerk takes some notes but looks bemused. The British boy is beside us. He hopes the British consulate staff can help him find a job. How likely that is, in a country where employment opportunities are scarce, he doesn't know, and the staff there are not encouraging.

"Oh well, I'll head for Libya," he says. He has heard that work exists in the oilfields.

At least we can tell the young man in the consulate where we will stay for the first night, the International Youth Hostel Association building in Tunis. That is some certainty before we launch ourselves into the unknown.

The hostel in Tunis is in a village a few miles out of town, and we travel to it by bus. We expect to find travellers like us from other countries, and here we can cook and find information.

It is a former mansion with a small freshwater swimming pool and we dive straight in. It is such a delight to be cool. And then we sit beside the pool, thinking about where we are. Overlooking orange trees and oxen ploughing a field. On the tip of Africa. In an Islamic world.

"*Français, Français!*" call out the little children as we walk through the nearby village looking for a shop. What else could we be, two pale-faced girls wearing denim skirts which show their legs below the knee, but French?

With our Tunisian money, we manage to buy spaghetti, cheese, eggs, vegetables and even wine. "*Merci, mesdames*," says the shopkeeper. "*Vous allez d'où?*" Where are you from?

We tell him we are from *Angleterre*. The women shoppers look at us curiously, smiling over the scarves that cover the lower half of their faces. Mary and I want to make friends with women in this world into which we have plunged. Their clothing that shuts them off from curious gazes is as strange to us as ours must be to them: we who show shamelessly, fearlessly, our legs to the world, and who don't cover our straw-coloured hair.

No Shoes
Tunis, 29–30 July 1965

In the hostel are many adventurous hitchhiking young people from other lands: Danes, Swedes, Tunisians, Germans, Swiss and British. In the company of Gerry and Ralph, two English boys from London who had also heard there is work to be found in North Africa, we visit the *medina*, the great market, in Tunis. My diary:

> *It was full of little shops selling most interesting things including lovely Arab antique jewellery, big coloured rugs, strange seeds and spices and incense. My shoes finally broke, so I went barefoot.*

Two English-speaking Tunisian boys befriend the four of us. "Would you like to visit the mosque?" They have guessed correctly. "But we thought only Moslems could enter a mosque?" we ask. In their company, it seems to be acceptable. My diary:

> *The others took their shoes off and we went in. It was very cool and quiet and dark. A few men were squatting, praying. One was trying to sleep and scratching away at his fleas. I kept imagining a shady personage hiding behind a pillar with a sharpened sword ready to pounce on us because we were Christians. But as we are not really practising Christians perhaps it didn't matter. Much of the mosque was still being built, the stones all being hand carved.*

All six of us make our way next to the sea on a local train, passing by the ruins of Carthage. We swim in our clothes as the sun is starting to set over a rocky bay near Carthage. The water is cool and pleasant but, as we have nothing to dry ourselves on, we drip back to Tunis and take a bus to the hostel. I still have no shoes, but no-one seems to pay any attention.

The evening is so delightfully warm that Mary and I decide to sleep outdoors. My diary:

> *We collected our blankets and found a shady orange grove in the hostel garden. This is of course highly against regulations but it was too nice to sleep indoors in this tempting Arabic night. There was such a view of stars that I had never realised how large the sky is. We woke to find cows and children looking at us. A big fat Arab came padding along to ask us why we were sleeping in his orange grove. He said it would serve us right if his dog ate us. Apart from that he didn't seem very worried and let us be.*

Next day, Mary and I begin our first hitchhike alone in Africa. It is six weeks since the date of the military coup in Algeria, the country we are planning to cross on our journey to the Sahara, unsure of what we'll find but confidently moving on.

Another Frontier
Bône, Algeria, 31 July 1965

We make friends along the way, soon finding that almost everyone is kind to us. My diary:

> *We stopped for a strong hot Tunisian coffee at a roadside kiosk, and we were invited into a farm to drink. The women here all wore lovely red and yellow clothes, and had tattoos on their arms and faces. Cows walked in and out of the house and cow pats were drying on the roof for winter fuel. The women were baking unleavened bread and the mother gave us a flat, warm loaf.*
>
> *As we get closer to the Algerian frontier, the next car to stop contains two Americans.*

"Gee, what are two young ladies like you doing along this road?" the driver asks. He and his companion must think we look in need of a decent meal, and they take us to their caravan in a dry, brown, rocky valley.

"My goodness, real meat," says Mary, watching as they pile our plates with turkey, tomatoes, onions, bilberry sauce, sweet potatoes, spinach, peas and home-made bread and butter. It is all served with plenty of glasses of red wine, and finished off with coffee and biscuits.

They point to a sad-looking villa and outbuildings near their caravan. "Abandoned and neglected since the French left the country," they tell us. They are geologists. "We are here looking for new water supplies, boring as deep as 300 metres." While we eat, a great hot wind swirls along and fills the valley with clouds of brown dust. A dust storm? We've never seen anything like this in our green grassy homeland. We truly must be near the desert.

The kind men give us twenty decent American cigarettes each and drive us to the *poste frontière*, where we will leave the friendly land of Tunisia for Algeria with its new military government.

We have a timetable. The date is 31 July. Mary's twenty-first birthday is 30 August. We have exactly thirty days from today to reach the Sahara desert, which is our goal, and then return through Spain and France to the UK. It is essential for family harmony that Mary is home in Wiltshire on that day if she doesn't want to break her mother's heart.

Hitchhiking in Tunisia so far has been trouble-free for us. We will soon see what it will be like in Algeria.

After the Americans drop us off, we approach the Algerian border post. It takes hours and hours booking in and out of customs offices, but we are eventually allowed through. We get into conversation with a French man. He is driving in a comfortable car all the way to Algiers, and he agrees that we may go with him. How lucky we are – a distance of three hundred miles, 480 kilometres, safely, quickly. We start to travel across a landscape that we could never have imagined. My diary:

> We drove into huge fantastic Algerian mountains. The south slopes were baked limestone hills, dry slopes planted with corn, deep slanting gorges, and saw lots of country people on donkeys. Their settlements were of straw stacked huts or skin tents, and probably are just summer places because these hills get covered with snow in winter. The north facing slopes were quite heavily wooded with oak trees. We slept quite a bit in the car and drove until dark. We haven't seen any political demonstrations.

Our French driver tells us he is a medical delegate, and takes us as far as the town of Bône that first day. He finds himself a hotel but as there is no youth hostel, he allows us to sleep in his car.

CAMELS AND NOMADS
ALGIERS, 1 AUGUST 1965

The scenery of this North African country continues to astonish us. My diary:

> What a day, what a country! We've seen camels grazing loose on old gold cornfields; passed by the skin tents of pastoral nomads – tents stretched out low and shady on poles. We've passed real semi-desert country and a blazing hot wind has been rushing through the car all day. We've crossed high dry cracked mountains settled by nomad tribes up from the desert for the summer. We've seen many people in coloured costumes which are flowing and billowing in the wind. We stopped for water at a pure cool fountain where herdsmen were watering their straggly-legged sheep. We passed through the town of Constantine, perched high above a fantastic limestone gorge.

Our driver helps us to interpret what we see. He stops so that we can meet and mingle with the shepherds at the fountain and encourages us to take a photograph. A quick stop at a kiosk in Constantine enables us to buy coloured postcards to stick in our diaries, pictures of the city with a flimsy-looking bridge spanning the gorge, set amid a dry arid landscape. By the end of the day, we reach Algiers, where he drives us right to the door of the youth hostel near the sea front.

Boys In Algiers
Algiers, 1–3 August 1965

In the hostel, there is friendly company and young people who speak our language. Despite the dangers of recent political upheaval, as with us, nothing has deterred them from finding their way to Algiers. My diary:

> *There's only one other girl here, an American, and crowds of fantastic boys including two Irish and two English. We sat and chatted and the American girl gave us cheese and bread. We washed ourselves so clean we could hardly recognise ourselves.*

Our aim is to meet young Algerians. It doesn't take long. As we leave the hostel in the morning, things suddenly go to an extreme. As fair-haired girls who are obviously not Algerian, we are attracting attention. My diary:

> *The pestering chaps were like bees around us, so we ran down the street and they all ran after us. One young man overtook us. He spoke English, and we decided the best thing to do was to let him look after us.*

Hit the Road, Gals

Abdou Guermouche and his brother Bibeh take us to their family house in Boulevard Salah Bouakouir.

"*Maman, deux anglaises,*" Abdou says to his mother. Two English girls. She accepts these unexpected friends of her sons courteously. At least we are cleaner today than we had been yesterday, and our hair is combed. But the boys can't be happy until they have sorted out our footwear. My shoes had broken while I was in Tunis market, and I hadn't replaced them. Since then, Mary's have collapsed too, and we are both going barefoot.

"To the market, come along," says Abdou. He and Bibeh take us to a shop, where they buy us each a pair of Algerian *espadrilles*. These are rope-soled slippers with blue cotton tops. Cool, comfortable and just what we like. Local clothing. Lots of people wear them. We feel quite in the fashion.

The boys are clearly not from a poor family, and next we go to their own private student flat. They impress us with their multilingual skills, fluent in both Arabic and French, and able to speak English with us. They write some beautiful Arabic script in my diary, incomprehensible to me but so impressive.

It is not long before they let us know they think that unaccompanied young English girls must want to enjoy the fruits of love. My diary:

All afternoon, between listening to records, we needed to explain our ideas about faire l'amour, and they propounded numerous of their opinions which always resulted with the same conclusion.

"We know some Swedish girls," they tell us. "Swedish girls love Algerian boys."

"We don't, in the way that you mean," we assure them. They explain that the Swedish girls are very emancipated. So why aren't we? They take us to visit the Swedish girls, who can see that we need feeding. They give us a delicious meal, which includes French bread, cheese and butter.

Together we all go to a beach to cool down. Swimming, right in the heart of Algiers! But between that and long walks around the harbour area, we are tired, and ready to end the day's activities.

The boys tell us we can stay the night at their flat. We'd like to do this, and we explain our rules, to which they agree. We collect our things from the youth hostel and spend the evening listening to music in their flat. Some others arrive, their brothers, a friend or two. They drop in and out. There is some guitar playing, and after the long walks we'd had during the day, and with the constant effort of speaking in French, I soon fall asleep on rugs on the floor. I have several visitations during the night, which I manage to keep at bay, as does Mary. In the morning we wake to the sound of enchanting Arabic instrumental music and songs from their record player. We would love to learn some, if it wasn't quite so difficult. The hospitable and cheerful Abdou and Bibeh see us on our way, exchanging friendly feelings, and we begin hitchhiking in the hot sun, westward, towards Morocco.

Domestic Harem
Les Attafs, 4 August 1965

At the end of the afternoon, we are given a lift by a lorry driver who invites us to his home in the small town of Les Attafs. He is a polite and slender young man who has been speaking to us in French. His name is Bounedjar Tahar Ben Ali. We are happy to accept because here in his house we will learn about family life in rural Algeria.

To enter, we pass through a wall into an enclosed courtyard surrounded by many rooms. A hush falls on the people inside as we arrive.

His wife is young and shyly hides behind her scarf when we talk to her. She speaks only a little French. There are many attractive children running around, one of whom seems to be a little servant. An elderly grandmother is squatting cross-legged by the door of her room.

We are honoured guests. This means that a chicken must be chased, caught, tortured and killed in our honour. The kitchen is baking hot, with food in large round wooden bowls being mixed up by the women. There is a huge baking oven for bread.

The evening meal preparations take some time, during which we chat with the young woman of the household, and her friend who arrives. She is dressed in a more European style. We compare our clothing. They are interested in our denim skirts, and we in their ankle-length divided pantaloons. We check and feel the fabrics.

"*Pantalons, pour vous?*" one of them enquires. "Pantaloons for you?" Mary looks pleased and gestures her agreement. A cotton skirt and a hand-worked sewing machine are brought out. Before long, Mary is wearing the comfortable divided trousers, which allow for easy walking and bending, and have a modesty opening for squatting while toileting. This is a wonderful and useful present. Mary smiles her pleasure. In return, we are able to offer some aspirin from our first aid kit to the young wife, who shows by gestures that she suffers from headaches.

A friend of the lorry driver, husband of the young friend, arrives. He is a large man, rotund and strong-looking. As the slow meal-making preparations continue, we are able to observe life in this household. My diary:

> *Talk about dominated women and cave men dragging them round by the hair. Well, it's like that here. The women look to their husbands' every command, even cease laughing when he appears and run to do his bidding. The women were all gay and cheerful with us, then along comes a husband and it changes to demureness and fear. Yet it seems to be respect*

and admiration too. Perhaps there's an element in a woman's make up that enjoys being totally subservient and inferior and makes it alright if they've never known anything else. But give me emancipation.

When the meal is ready, we are invited to the low-legged table. My diary:

It was couscous first, like semolina with butter or cheese mixture, and it tasted delicious. Mary then proceeded to eat the chicken's legs, the one that had been running around when we entered the courtyard. I ate chips and fried peppers. With this we ate sweet pink melon, and it all tasted lovely together. But we had to eat with the men, not the women.

Further hospitality is being arranged. My diary:

You read in wild exotic travel books about situations like this, but when it actually happens to you – almost – it takes some believing. They had all been great to us, let us do anything, look at anything, when next a big bed with satin covers was being prepared for us in a separate part of the house. The only trouble was that the men spent a lot of time around this bed and as night fell we began to wonder exactly what was expected of us. We weren't really sure if we were expected to spend the night with them – these were two young married men. The wives appeared to take the whole procedure for granted. In fact they were so calm that we thought we must be mistaken.

Then these two men changed their clothes. One put on a pair of clean coloured underpants which the grandmother got from a cupboard, and the other a loose Arab gown transparent enough for us to see what he did and didn't wear underneath.

We looked at them. Our host was small and kind, and we could manage him. But the other was huge, and looked very strong, and we didn't fancy a fight.

It was difficult to decide what to do because you never know how these people will react. It may be so rude to turn down their generous ideas of hospitality that they might murder us. It was very dark, and drums were being tapped somewhere in the village.

The women and children were sitting around, talking with us, all in our best French. We decided to tell them that we wanted none of this. They were surprised but didn't seem to mind. The younger woman, who spoke most French, went off laughing to her husband who was the large man.

Presently the men reappear looking rather abashed, and a bed is made up for us with rugs on the floor in the grandmother's room, while she slept across the doorway.

We let out sighs of relief. Now we're lying ready to sleep, having just been spared an Arabian nightmare. It's quiet and dark in here, with soft voices of people who sit around, and the tom-tom drums are beating in the village. But at least we can sleep in peace tonight.

Dancing
Sebdou, 5–6 August 1965

Next morning, our host lines up the children in front of the sunflowers by the wall so that we may take a photograph of them. But, when we encourage his wife and mother to join the group, he adamantly refuses. We demur but are in no position to insist.

Now Mary and I are having a first-hand experience of the Islamic lifestyle. My diary:

All day we've been thinking about Arab life and the treatment of the women. It seems strange, and a waste, that once a girl becomes a woman she has to become ashamed of her body and cover it all up. We saw some extreme cases today where only one eye and the hands and feet were exposed to daylight. The father this morning would not let any of the women be on the photograph, and we thought that very unkind.

It is very difficult not to look at the lives of these people from the point of view of a western European. We seem to naturally absorb ideas of equality and freedom, and we think restraining and curbing freedom is bad. I enjoy my own freedom and don't like to think others can't stand up for themselves.

Yet we are finding that the women in this land are exceptionally kind to us, as strangers. As we continue our hitchhiking towards Morocco, Mary looks almost like a local as she walks along wearing her *pantalons* and *espadrilles*, and carrying her pack on her back.

Along the way, we enter a village shop. It is really no more than a room in a flat-roofed house, with a refrigerator in the corner. Mary loves milk, and she sees a pyramid-shaped carton. It costs her a few pence, and when we are out on the road she eagerly nips off the corner and takes a big slurp.

"Aaaagh…" she yells, spitting it out on the dusty road. It was some sour, unfamiliar kind of treated milk, and her pennies have been wasted.

In the town of Sebdou, we enter a village shop and are soon in conversation with a veiled woman. "*Venez chez moi*," she beckons. Come to my house.

"*Je m'appelle Mme Bendahmane Fatiha*," she introduces herself. My name is Madame Bendahmane Fatiha. We enter the door of a small walled enclosure and are soon surrounded by children and neighbours. It is a house of warmth and feminine friendliness. The men are somewhere else. We are embraced with kindness and given endless little glasses of mint tea.

We decide to do our own share of the entertaining. I play "The

Gay Gordons", a Scottish dance tune, on my little mouth organ. Fatiha's five children gaze in astonishment as Mary, dressed in her Arab *pantalons*, leaps and bounds and whoops, using neat heel-and-toe footwork. "*Encore, encore!*" They know those French words.

Now Fatiha and the other young girls decide they will show us the correct, elegant way to dance. Singing and chanting rhythmically together, they expose their midriffs in wriggles and side-to-side movements. Aha, we think, belly dancing! This is certainly a new experience for us. Mary copies, and they encourage her. I envy her flexibility, and she is a quick learner.

"*Bien, bien. Elle danse bien*," they agree with smiles. She dances well.

We are rewarded in the evening with a meal of couscous, fried peppers and chicken. It seems that inside this home at least the women are free among themselves to look after the strangers, and we are put to sleep in a dreamy, comfortable bed with satin covers.

Moroccan Song
Oujda, Morocco, 6 August 1965

Next day, we get lifts through the limestone gorges near Tlemcen, and arrive at the Moroccan border. At the frontier post, we line up in one queue after another to allow the officials to check our passports and examine our baggage. It takes two hours before we step through into Morocco.

It has taken us eight days to cross Algeria, a country that has had revolutions and turmoil, and yet has been kind to us. We have encountered no violence. We've been welcomed on our way first by the French medical delegate, then by Abdou and Bibeh in Algiers, followed by the too-familiar household in Les Attafs and finally by Fatiha and her children in Sebdou.

Once settled in at the youth hostel in the Moroccan border town of Oujda, we work out our finances and discover that we've crossed Algeria on one shilling each. And we've experienced the unforgettable kindness of Islamic people to strangers.

All the way through Tunisia and Algeria we have heard the haunting, horizontal melodies of Arabic music. They feel oriental, unfamiliar, and we find it hard to hum or tap our feet to the tricky rhythms. But we really want to learn a song. We have heard on the radios of various vehicles a song that to our ears has become *Moushki ferya ya habibi*. A friendly man at Oujda youth hostel agrees to teach it to us. He is a schoolteacher, which perhaps makes him patient with slow learners. We do our best with the tune and the words, and the cry of longing, *aaaaaamel iiiiiih*. The only phrase we really understand is *ya habibi*, my beloved. That is easy enough to remember. *Moushki ferya ya habibi* may become useful to our futures as geography teachers, we think, and we practise singing as we trundle along the roads in the hot sunshine.

City Of The South
Marrakesh, 9–10 August 1965

It takes us three days to hitchhike from Oujda, near the Algerian border, to the city of Marrakesh. Of the many marvellous places we have seen so far in our North African travels, nothing can compare with this.

We are sitting in a little restaurant overlooking the great market place of Marrakesh, the Jemaa el-Fna. The colourful people in the markets, the scents of cooking with herbs and spices, musicians playing on drums, storytellers surrounded by rapt people, watersellers with decorated hats, women in brightly coloured costumes as well as those in full covering. All the stalls are lit with tiny lanterns amid the warm darkness of the Moroccan night. My diary:

> *There were water sellers ringing bells. Snake charmers and drummers and all kinds of entertainers in the huge square. We've never seen anything like it. Mary and I were hungry again, hadn't eaten since last night. We ate soup, eggs, chips, followed by treacle cake and delicious mint tea. Sat on the terrace overlooking the square and it cost us three shillings each. It was worth a fortune.*

Along the way, we'd spent one night in a shed on the outskirts of Fez, and the next in an empty house in Casablanca. We'd bumped into Ralph and Gerry, the English boys we'd met in Tunis, and who were supposed to be going to Libya but had changed their plans. For two days, we had split up and hitchhiked in boy/girl pairs. It had been easier for the boys but slowed us down. On the third day, we had decided to separate and make our own way to Marrakesh.

It is so easy to make friends here. Soon we are chatting with two boys, a Belgian and a Tunisian. The latter lives here, and he invites us to stay. He assures us his family will make us welcome. My diary:

We went by horse taxi, and it was exciting clip-clopping through all the streets crowded with people. How much we'll miss these Arabian nights when we get home. We were taken to a house with an open-air courtyard in the backstreets of the medina. It is decorated inside with hand-carved tiles and arches, painted like an Arab mosque. Very lovely. And now we're sitting listening to Arab music, and the boys are playing cards.

But the next day, the romance dies down a little. My diary:

Today we had Moroccan treatment. We became like Arab girls, and we had a glimpse of what life must be like for the dominated half of the population. What a difference between say the Italian way of courting a girl, and the Arab way. Italians bow at your feet, do everything you want, flatter you, charm you, become your slave. Arab men almost drag you round by the hair. You become their slave. All day long we didn't have the slightest choice in anything we did. We were taken here, and left there, and we spent a great part of the day waiting for cousins and being patient.

We were entertained two times to fantastic meals. Their food is an absolute delight to eat. Various mixtures of burning hot peppers, strange vegetables, couscous, chips, eggs, salads, all spicy.

But it took literal forcing to get those chaps to agree to take us to the medina. We were torn between wanting to feel like Arab girls for a day and wanting to stop these men being so bossy and presumptuous towards us. How do women feel having their every action dictated to them? It must be irritating even if it has been like that all their lives.

Eventually we do manage to persuade the boys to accompany us to the *medina*. It would have been very tricky to manage without them because we'd certainly have got lost in the endless maze of alleyways and we have little experience of prices or bargaining. My diary:

> As we have spent hardly any money so far on all our travels, we decided we could afford to give ourselves £5 each to buy some things for ourselves and for presents.
> We both wanted Arab women's clothes, so in the medina the boys helped us choose our djellabas. These are long loose garments with a hood, and the women wear them with yashmaks, scarves covering the nose and lower face.
> Mary chose a grey djellaba with an orange scarf, and I a greenish-blue djellaba with a pink scarf. We also bought hand carved wooden spoons to take home and a tom-tom drum such as you hear everywhere here which cost about two shillings and threepence.
> Everything seems hand made by individual craftsmen and their families. We've seen a weaving loom, a complicated affair which employed two people and wove beautiful colour blankets. We've seen tailors' shops where the whole family, men and boys only, were sewing up women's djellabas. We've seen hand sewing of bright yellow shoes that a lot of men wear; and hand beaten brasses and coppers, hand wood carving and furniture making.

We are later taken to the house of one of the friends, wearing our new *djellabas* and *yashmaks*, playing the part of subdued Moroccan girls. My diary:

> We were waited on hand and foot during the supper, the men lounging around and calling the girls of the family to their service all the time. There were three of them, all with eastern Rajah-Caliph-type faces, which began to glow with

oriental ideas as it grew later. *The Arab music wailed as we sat around the low table and all ate couscous by hand from a huge plate in the centre of the table. One of the boys began dancing with Mary, with a shaking head and expressionless face. The atmosphere felt a thousand years old. The only difference was that we had to bring it back to 1965 by insisting that we didn't sleep alone with these boys in a house full of carpets and cushions, in an open-air courtyard where the fountain was playing in the moonlight.*

These men tell any lie they feel like to get you to do what they want, and if you question what they have said, more lies or excuses pass it off. It took some doing to get back to the house and family where we'd been last night. We marched back through the silent deserted streets beside niggled chaps, doing as many jigsaw patterns to get unpaired as they did to get us paired. It was a battle of wits.

ATLAS CROSSING
OUARZAZATE, 11 AUGUST 1965

We are longing to ride on camels over the sand dunes. After two nights in Marrakesh, it is time to head south over the gigantic Atlas Mountains. I am reminded of a little verse I had made up as part of a poem at school at age eleven:

Atlas was a giant who held up the sky.
To give it to Hercules did he try.
But Hercules could not be tricked.
He said: To do it you've been picked.

Our first destination south from Marrakesh is Ouarzazate, where we know we should find a Moroccan youth hostel. My diary:

We crossed a mountain pass at 7000 feet. What dry bare mountains, not a speck of grass or plants, just dry earth and cracked rocks. Sometimes there were little streams in the valleys, and beside them were bushes covered in bright pink flowers. The villages were all flat-roofed, and made of mud bricks. It was cloudy in part, and we even had a few spots of rain. The scent of wet ground made me want to be back in England for a few minutes.

In the hostel at Ouarzazate, we met some French boys who had found a chameleon, and we made it change colour by putting it on different coloured clothes.

Caliph's Palace
Agdz, 12 August 1965

We are becoming a little closer to the Sahara. My diary:

In the morning, we had a ride in a cement lorry. We passed lots of castles or fortresses built, like the houses, of sun-baked mud bricks. Our lorry drivers took us for a Berber meal at a desert transport café. We ate pancake things like pizza, with meat stew for the carnivores and eggs for me, followed by lots of mint tea.

We arrived at 2 pm in Agdz and found it was market day. All the tribesmen were down from the hills selling sheep, wool and flour. They are very tall and finely built, loose-limbed, and they walk like kings. Some of the men in their flowing white djellabas and turbans carry dangerous-looking swords and sabres. Sometimes they are mounted on horse or mule, looking fearsome. The women do not show themselves much, but they don't cover their faces. They wear gaily coloured assortments of headgear, skirts and blouses, and they carry their babies on their backs.

Mary and I bought a donkey pannier each made of palm leaves to carry our things in. But there was no luck getting a lift any further. We waited until 4.30 pm, and not a vehicle passed. It is going to be difficult to hitchhike into the desert, and we can see that the road has disintegrated into a stony track. So we decided to call on the Caliph of the town, a person who is a sort of mayor.

"Bonjour. Bienvenue chez moi!" he said when he opened the door to his impressive palace at the top of the hill amid a palm grove. Welcome to my home!

He presented us to his satin-dressed wife who was seated cross-legged on low cushions. A servant brought us crispy almond cakes and mint tea. His children showed us round their exotic garden with fig trees and date palms, and later we were served a huge meal of pasta and potato omelette. I am writing this in a bedroom with a view through the open-air arched window of the Caliph's palace. We are looking over the palm trees which grow beside the dried-up valley of the River Draa which winds south towards the Sahara.

Not In Summer
Zagora, 13 August 1965

We have heard that cars don't go to the desert in the summer, and we find this out for ourselves. My diary:

We sat around until 5 pm today, and about three cars passed. They were all full, and they all came back because the road was too bad. A Frenchman joined us who was hitching in the same direction. At one time along came a car full of English people who had turned back northward, and who complained about the horrible heat of the desert.

At midday, we'd ordered a delicious lunch of omelette with cheese and wine. We love sitting at low tables and having one big plate for everyone, and eating by hand. We sat there and waited for the noise of a vehicle heading our way which could be heard long before it arrived.

Eventually three Moroccans arrived in a Land Rover-type vehicle going to Zagora, and the Frenchman, Mary and I piled in. What better way to travel to the Sahara than in a jeep with local people! We passed more of the high fortified mud brick houses with busy Berber people around. The road was just a track of dry sand and stones. It took well over three hours to do 100 kilometres, or 60 miles. Bump bump bump all the time. Clouds of dust followed us.

Mary's notebook has her own perspective:

We travel down the right side of the Draa valley, palm trees following the river, backed by high mountains. The jeep swings and bumps and bounces over the roads. We pass workmen breaking up rocks on the side of the road, numerous mud fortresses like villages, women dressed in black robes edged with reds and yellows. A group of fine-looking old men were sitting on their haunches in their white robes and turbans. We continue to marathon-ride over the bumps, and sing all the Scottish songs we can think of, and Keep Right on to the End of the Road, because we are going to the end of the road on the map. It rains! Glorious rain, hardly more than a few drops, but we stretch our hands out of the window, feeling it lovely against our dust-covered skin. It gets dark, and we pass many donkeys on the road, the men always riding and the women walking behind. We decide it wouldn't do for us.

We pass a sign saying Zagora 26 km and at last see the lights marking the entrance to the town. Straight away we met a friend of the driver who took us to the schoolroom to drink mint tea in candlelight.

While we sit there in the early evening dusk, a tall man in a white turban arrives carrying a dish containing cool water and dates, which he offers to us, the strangers. We are very much moved. After being offered cool water in which to wash, we dress in our *djellebas* and are given camp beds in which to sleep on the balcony. Drums are beating from the town, and we are left in peace to sleep.

Direction Timbuktu
Mhamid, 14 August 1965

Zagora is a place from which roads lead off in different directions. As we leave, we see a sign that shows Tagounite as thirty-four kilometres and Mhamid eighty-four kilometres, our destination. It also shows Hassi-Beida 124 kilometres, Le Lac d'Irike 300 kilometres and, most amazing of all, Tombouctou thirty-two *jours*! Timbuktu, thirty-two days. This must mean across the desert, and surely by camel caravan!

We are at the final stretch of our journey to the Sahara, to Mhamid at the very end of the road. The camels are waiting for us, we feel sure, and perhaps the glamorous sheikh of my desert song daydreams. My diary:

We sat beside the road at the outskirts of Zagora in the morning prepared to wait all day for a lift. We looked at the road to the desert. There was nothing but dry land, rocks and mountains, with a sort of stony path going through it.

I visited a Berber home while Mary sat by the roadside and wrote her diary. Almost all the women had babies on their back. They gave me a strange white soup and fresh dates. I went back then to Mary, prepared to wait for hours, and almost straight away along comes a jeep. "Vous allez à Mhamid?" With disbelief at our good luck, we climbed in.

Along the way, the men stopped at the souk, the market, at Tamegroute. We did our own shopping, buying a palm-leaf fan each, and admiring the beautiful antique-looking silver jewellery.

When we left the market, the jeep was piled to overflowing. Four men were in the front, and in the open back a little black boy, rush mats, bread, grapes, four chickens and us. We made the chickens comfortable in one of our palm donkey paniers, and we hung on as the jeep jolted towards the desert.

The road was barely discernible among the flat stones of the plain as we left Tamegroute. We got lost a few times, and the driver asked a wandering shepherd which way to go. He indicated that we had to cross the dry Draa river, the thundering waters of which must have been responsible in the past for this immense desert valley. The jeep rattled on to the stony bed, crossed half a dozen puddles full of leeches, and away once again from the palm trees. We crossed the next huge range of mountains and down into another irrigated palm grove around which we saw the first sand dunes of the Sahara.

Arriving at an irrigation station, Mary and I were able to climb a ladder and soak ourselves in the water tank, about six feet square and three feet deep. Then we walked along the irrigation channel about ten feet above the ground.

Near the water tank is a little house made of palm branches. Shyly, a young woman with a tiny baby on her back makes us welcome. She and her husband are wearing the blue cotton attire of the desert peoples. We are served many cups of mint tea. She is not as reserved in front of the men as some of the women we'd seen on our travels. Before long, she shows us her beautiful, best clothes.

Kindly, she encourages us to try on her outfit. I am first. A dark, almost navy-blue dress is wound in place by black bands and tied up in red sashes, and a coloured scarf is wound around my head. And then her darling little baby is tied on my back! Mary is dressed after me. We feel these are a lot of clothes to wear in the hot weather, but perhaps they get used to it. Our common language being French, of which we all know but little, communication is through smiles and gestures. But we learn that our Blue Woman friend who is seventeen years old was married at the age of fourteen. No-one had seemed particularly surprised by that.

Now we are close to where the sands of the Sahara may kiss a moonlit sky, and where my daydreams of a handsome sheikh and desert breezes whisp'ring may perhaps be a reality.

The drivers of the jeep move along on towards Mhamid. At last, we see the walls of what looks like a military fortress with a tower rising above the sand. That is all there is, a huge empty expanse of sand separating the fortress from the flat roofs of a tiny village nearby. The driver of the jeep takes us to the entrance of fortress. We have learned about caliphs and their tradition of hospitality in Agdz.

"*Faites comme chez vous*," says the fat-bellied, balding Caliph of Mhamid. "Make yourselves at home."

He took us into his house. A soldier produces the inevitable, delicious mint tea, and we explain that we would like to ride on the Caliph's camels. With sparkling eyes, he informs me that we can do this tonight, and that I am the Calipha now. He is wearing shorts, with a loose T-shirt over a bare torso, nothing like the romantic sheikh in *The Desert Song*.

We are surprised to see that in this remote, almost waterless area he has a small swimming pool. It is not much larger than an average living room, and the water is grey-brown, only a metre or so deep. Nevertheless, it is water, and a luxury here at the edge of the desert. He must be an important man. My diary:

> *We were soon cooling off in the swimming pool. But he kept chasing me and grabbing me, and once he chased me so much that I screamed continuously so that his guards would hear. Then he went off in a huff, and it took him half an hour to forgive me!*
>
> *It was too dark to go out on the camels tonight anyway, so we cooked our own supper in his kitchen, a strange company, two jeep drivers, the Caliph, Mary and me. To relieve some tension, we decided I would play The Gay Gordons on my mouth organ. Mary taught the Caliph a highland fling in the kitchen, and he suddenly lost all his importance in our eyes as his belly swung from side to side.*

After our meal, everyone moved out to sleep on the balcony, Mary and I staying as close together as possible. Mary wrote a little ditty in her notebook:

> *While the moon her watch was keeping*
> *The Caliph's eyes were keenly peeping*
> *Whilst we were soundly sleeping.*
>
> The next morning, dozens of drowned big black beetles were floating on the surface of the swimming pool and had to be scooped out with a long-handled net.

Camels At Last
Mhamid, 15 August 1965

All my romantic fantasies of a handsome sheikh are abandoned. Still, we have managed to get to the Sahara and are close to our ambition to ride over the sand dunes on the Caliph's camels. He knows this. It is his bargaining point. My diary:

> All day long, the amorous Caliph and the one man remaining were pestering us. I was truly fed up, and at one point I thought, "Blow your camel ride. I'm off." I packed my bag. But Mary, diplomatic as ever, managed to charm them and change the situation, and it was agreed that we could go to the camels. The arrangements were being made, and my bad temper soon changed.

Mary's notebook:

> While we waited, we collected matchboxes full of Sahara sand, and then organised a salad for lunch. We swam in the Caliph's pool, practising our diving, followed by a discussion with the Caliph about our fiancés en Angleterre.

This ruse about our faithfulness to imaginary fiancés in England is intended to explain our resistance to the charms of those who would woo us. I don't really think it works, but it keeps the discussion going. Finally we are taken to the camels. My diary:

> First of all, I nearly fell off when the camel stood up, and I wobbled dangerously when the camel started running. It felt so high up on the top of the hump. Mary mounted hers, and an assigned Blue Man who was acting as our guide rode on the third. Very unfortunately, Mary was feeling ill, today of all days, and the camel's movement made her feel worse.

> *Before long, the man who was leading her camel turned back with her. On I went alone with my Blue Man guide.*
>
> *We passed a waterhole with donkeys and stopped to drink. Then we came to an astonishing building operation – the making of a dam across the river bed which is dry for three quarters of the year. It was built "Egyptian pyramid style", rows of people walking along in lines, carrying stones in their hands, and an overseer with a whip.*
>
> *The remaining two camels passed on, making shadows of us in the sand. We went right into the sand dunes, mounting and riding over them. The camels' enormous feet didn't leave much mark in the sand. They were smelling their direction, noses to the wind. I wanted it to last longer. I was so enjoying the peace away from the amorous Caliph. But back we went towards the palace. I was told the camels can last about four days in this heat without drinking. They were given dry dates and oats before they retired to their tethers in the sand.*

We had achieved our dream, sort of, but poor Mary's was cut short as she returned to the fortress. Her notebook:

> *The Caliph had a little hospital in his palace where they gave me three lots of tablets, white, black and pink. Then he turned up with Pepsi-cola, and said that I must cool down. I paddled in the pool while he poured cold water over my head. That wasn't the end of it. His remedy for weak muscles which he demonstrated: lie on your stomach and let a Blue Man pull your muscles away from the bone. And for a sick stomach, lie on a glass for five minutes. A joke! Still, you must experience local customs. Drank milk for supper and then slept soundly.*

Water From England
High Atlas, 16-17 August 1965

In exactly two weeks' time, we must be back in England for Mary's family celebration of her twenty-first birthday. Now we are in Mhamid and we need some good luck. Our bags are packed. Not a car or a jeep or a lorry is anywhere around. We're listening and watching, and looking forward to being away from the hospitality of the Caliph. A large and busy group of men are at work between the fortress and the village. We can see that they are making mud bricks, and we want to learn how it is done. These tall thin men, wearing white or black turbans, allow us to join in.

My diary:

> *We jumped in the mud and tramped it up and down with water. Then we rolled it into pats with straw and put it in moulds. We were covered in mud and enjoying this very much when we spied, near the flat little houses of the village, a white European car.*

I raced barefoot over the hot sand to investigate. The retired couple from southern England were shortly going back to Zagora and they could take us! Great news. We all went to the souk in the little mud brick village where Mary and I purchased a packet of green tea to make with mint.

Before long we are squashed up in the back of the car, leaving Mhamid behind, with its camels and its mystified Caliph, who despite it all had to come to terms with two wandering inexplicable English girls.

The couple are birdwatchers, and they spot citril finches, to their great delight.

"Are you thirsty?" they ask us at one point. Of course. We are always thirsty. The woman opens the boot and we see large water containers which they'd carried all the way from England.

In Zagora, we separate from the English couple. We spot a parked lorry loaded with crates of empty bottles. It is pointing in the direction of Marrakesh, and we negotiate a ride with the driver, leaving at 7 pm. Mary's notebook:

I went with a man to an irrigated date palm garden, under-cultivated with pomegranate trees with the fruit growing on them. I managed to pick a few. Bridget meanwhile invited a blind man in for tea. He played his pipe while we sang and danced. When our lorry came, we made a bed on boxes of bottles with a tarpaulin, blankets and the driver's *djellaba*, and started off. It was impossible to sleep. We had to hold onto chains to stop bumping off. There were numerous men sitting by the road, hitching, but the driver wouldn't pick them up unless they had some money. We stopped at Agdz to give a message to the Caliph, and then it was clear we will be stopping soon to sleep for a bit. Good. I'll be able to have Bridge's party on the top of the lorry.

We stopped on the edge of a precipice in a gale-force wind. With the help of the driver, I managed to light the candle for Bridge's 21st, and held it on the packet of biscuits while I sang Happy Birthday to You. Then we ate the pomegranates and the biscuits. Bridge had a few interruptions while I am thinking all the time of being on the edge of the precipice in the gale-force wind.

The disgruntled driver, unsuccessful in his seduction and marriage proposal, drops us off thirty kilometres from Marrakesh.

Return To Europe
Marrakesh to Málaga, 18–19 August 1965

Our route is now north from Marrakesh across Morocco to the Mediterranean coast, where we will cross from Africa into Europe. The *Mappa Mundi* in Hereford Cathedral shows the Pillars of Hercules as two columns on an island at the entrance the Mediterranean Sea. It labels the Rock of Gibraltar with *Terminus Africe* on one side and *Terminus Europe* on the other. We will be returning to the known western world.

As we travel northward in an overnight lift, the driver stops to sleep for a while. My diary:

I'd been riding on the back of the van because I'd felt a bit queer, so I slept in the fresh air with six chickens. I heard the usual, "Non M'sieu, ce n'est pas bon pour moi d'embrasser tout les garçons dans les voitures," from Mary inside the cabin with the young driver.

She is saying in her best French, "No sir, it is not good for me to embrace all the young men in the vehicles." The driver crossly dumps us beside the road near Tétouan, where we must find our way to the ferryboat for Spain. My diary:

We laughed at ourselves because we looked so funny. We were wearing our djellabas, we had three donkey baskets full of drums, dates, wooden spoons etc and our rucksacks. But by the end of the day, we weren't laughing very much. Crying more like.

We soon discovered that Ceuta, where we were catching the boat, was in Spanish Morocco, and we had to cross the frontier. How quickly everything changes from Arabic to European. We were seeing Spanish people, fat women once more, and beautiful girls, and hearing Pss Pss Rubia again. We dashed to catch the boat to Algeciras, but all the tickets for third class were sold and we hadn't enough cash for second class. We charged away from the ticket office just as the boat was leaving. The ticket man said, "No posible" as we pushed past him and jumped onto the boat, saying "Si si posible," and stayed there until the gangplank was pulled up and they had to take us. Eventually they charged us something between third and second class.

On the boat we were joined by a crowd of French and Moroccan boys. We got out our instruments, drums, spoons and pipes and sat singing, watching the coast of Africa fading away. It wasn't long before Gibraltar appeared. Mary was really looking forward to a big meal of bacon and eggs at Smokey Joe's café.

We are between the continents, a crossing of attitude as well as of land. Once off the boat, we make our way around the coastal road along the short distance to Gibraltar. My diary:

Dressed as we were in our djellabas, we looked so picturesque with all our souvenirs that some tourists took photos of us. We were very happy, and hitched around towards Gibraltar. The bacon and eggs were calling.

We met an English policeman in his uniform and helmet, and there were lots of people speaking English around. We were shown to the passport bureau. First question from a steely-eyed policeman, "How much money have you?" "Five pounds," we said. "Let me see it! This won't do. I'm afraid I cannot let you onto Gibraltar." We were very surprised. "Why not?" "Because that is not enough money to see you through, and that is all there is to it! You can't go through." All the time, his cold grey eyes glared at us, and we hated him. We felt what it was like to be turned away by your own countrymen and sent back to Spain where the Spanish frontier police tried their best to cheer us up.

We tried every way to get in. Mary so much wanted her bacon and eggs, and I too was looking forward to an English cup of tea. But all we got was sarcastic looks and, "They're back again." We understood very well why the Spanish would like to get the British out of Gibraltar.

We waited around until 3 pm in a last vain hope of getting on to the rock and in the end began hitchhiking towards Málaga. There were a lot of young men hitching so we offered our services and split up with two Americans. They didn't know what to make of us, but they did agree.

Out for experiences, I guess. Mine was an intelligent superpsychological intellectual called John. He proceeded to start talking about the cultural soul of the states of America, emerging in a kind of unity through America's only natural creative force, modern jazz. He also talked about the book he was writing about a metamorphosis of camel/lion/child. Apart from all this, he was quite fun.

We travelled to Málaga together, passing lovely silver beaches, mountains and white villages. About 10 pm we met Mary and Ed outside the youth hostel which was full. So we decided to cheer ourselves up with a meal. We had salad, chips, meat, omelette and three bottles of wine which of course made me feel sleepy while having the opposite effect on Mary. We went to the beach and had a moonlight swim in the warm water. After that I went straight off to sleep in my blanket. The others were awake for hours, apparently, and two policemen came to chase them away but they didn't move. In the morning, we could see that the beach was filthy and full of flies.

Flamenco
Antequera, 20 August 1965

We part from the boys as they are heading for Granada and we to Córdoba. It had been during summer last year, 1964, that Mary, Chris and I had first visited Córdoba. My diary:

> *The lorry we are in was extremely slow. We had to climb very steep mountains from Málaga and the road wound for miles, in and out, to get up. It took hours to get about 20 kilometres, but the scenery was great. About midday we were passing through a small town where there were lots of horses, mules and cattle in fields, and crowds of people. A fair! We hopped out of the lorry and dumped our baggage. There were lots of gypsies and Spanish peasants. The gypsies were very curious and friendly to us. It is the usual blue eyes and fair hair business. We noticed some very handsome young men, tall, lean dark gypsies too. We realised we'd stumbled on a real Spanish fiesta, which we never saw properly before in all the five weeks we'd been in Spain last year. To make it better there weren't any tourists around, and all the people laughed and joked with us.*

Hit the Road, Gals

"Señoritas would like to ride on the horses?" they asked us. Of course we would. They took us for a little ride around and took each other's photos. Mary's blouse is now torn and ragged and all the gypsies thought this was very amusing. They didn't beg, only laughed when we said we had no money too, and pointed to Mary's blouse.

Before long, three Spanish boys arrived who spoke French, and told us about the fiesta. We forgot about going to Córdoba and decided to stay here for the night, and found a pensión with a room for seven shillings and sixpence. In the town, the girls were wearing lovely coloured dresses, many piled onto horse carts singing and clapping. We slept a little, enjoying the Spanish siesta, the boys Manuel and Ramon arranging to meet us in the evening.

First they took us off to the bullring to view the bulls for tomorrow's big fight. We watched these eight huge black bulls led into the ring, one by one, for everyone to see what the fight would be like tomorrow. As last year, we were torn between understanding bull fighting from a Spaniard's point of view and our natural sympathy towards those shiny, handsome black bulls.

Next we went to the fiesta proper, and because we had men with us we could gaze at everything in peace without the continuous Pss Pss Rubia. The fair was all clean and shining, everything cheap, lit with lights between the trees, and girls wearing those lovely dresses. We wanted to see the flamenco dancing. But these men, just as in Marrakesh, tell lies all the time to get you to go where they want, and persuaded us to go to the Chinese circus. It wasn't very Chinese. It was singing, dancing and legs. Everyone enjoyed it except me. After the circus, the boys said it was too late to see the dancing.

The men always want to take charge, it seems, and because we are their guests, we have allowed ourselves to be persuaded. But this is too much. We determine to look for some flamenco ourselves. My diary:

> We found a platform in the town square where everything seemed unorganised. People got up and performed as they felt like it, whirling, intricate steps, singing, stamping, playing guitar accompaniments. Some of them befriended us and showed Mary how to play castanets.

In return, we do "The Gay Gordons" together, arms around each other's shoulders, I trying as well as I can to play the tune on my harmonica at the same time. The dancing is so unlike their flamenco that they gaze in polite wonderment.

Not A Sex-Maniac
US Air Force base, 21–22 August 1965

Letters are waiting for us in Córdoba the next day, at the post office's *poste restante*. My diary:

Mary's mother had written to her, furious because she hadn't told her she was going to the desert. Trouble awaits us back at home. My mother had written, and Rosie posted me a pack containing twenty-one cards. We put them all around us as we ate our omelettes in a little cafétéria, as if we were having a party. "Se vende?" asks a customer. Are they for sale? "Happy birthday cards," we explain.

Our next lift takes us to Madrid. We get there about 10 pm. So that we could get away early next morning, we take a bus to the edge of the city and try to sleep on a building site. I have fallen ill, suffering terrific stomach pains, and am lying shivering on the ground while Mary tries to get a lift. Her notebook:

Three Americans stopped in their Volkswagen car. "Do you girls fancy coming for a drink?" "No thanks, we're just fine." "Hey, you know I can't bear to see you looking so cold. Let me find you a blanket." The driver gets out and pulls a blanket from the boot to go round Bridge. Somehow, we admit that we are tired, hungry and thirsty. "Why didn't you say so in the first place?" We explain the set-up. Three chaps, picking up two girls at three in the morning. "What do you think I am, a sex-maniac?" We decide to trust them. We were smuggled onto their American air force base, past the guards, the boys, names Jerry, Mick and Monkey, acting unconcernedly. They drove us up to their restaurant, where I had egg and chips with toast and butter, and coffee. Poor Bridge couldn't eat anything. After that, they prepared to put us back on the road, but then, doubtfully so that we wouldn't misunderstand them, said that we were quite welcome to the spare single bed in Jerry's room. They smuggled us to their sleeping quarters where Bridge soon fell asleep. But I showered and washed hair and clothes.

Monkey and Mike slept on the floor, with great arguments following about Monkey snoring.

The story continues with my diary:

We slept until 11 am, and I felt a little better. The boys showed us around the camp. It was like being in the USA, big flashy cars, modern buildings, well-planned highway and chrome-plated cafétérias. They took us for coffee, and we noticed how the black and the white men ate in separate tables. Also, something very strange to us was the piles of free comics which the men could take to read. We didn't know grown men read comics. After giving Mary a dazzling white shirt to replace her torn one, they drove us past the guards and onto the road. What gentlemen! They had seen two maidens in distress and wanted to help us. We had doubted them so unfairly.

They drive us twenty kilometres along our way, as we are heading for Pamplona and the crossing of the Pyrenees. We arrive near the border and I calculate that we have travelled a total of 700 miles, 1140 kilometres, through Spain in the last three days. We have crossed from the south to the north of Spain, encountered the unforgiving British in Gibraltar, tumbled into a fiesta and learned that the American Air Force has a base in Franco's Spain.

Now all we need to do is pass through France to Boulogne, cross the Channel, make our way to Mary's house in time for her twenty-first birthday, and face her mother.

Food In France
Pamplona to Boulogne, 22–25 August 1965

It is extraordinarily easy to cross France even though we have hardly any money. We get lifts over the Pyrenees in the rain to a youth hostel in St-Jean-Pied-de-Port, and after that another lift to Bordeaux. A French girl takes us to spend the night at her parents' house in the country. In Limousin, two handsome French men give us a lift and take us for a picnic in the woods along the way. An innocent picnic, with lots of cheese and meat for hungry girls. From there, one after another, two lorries take us to Paris. My diary:

> We got to Paris about 6 am where we were given two coffees free in a café by offering to exchange some Spanish cigarettes. We were in Boulogne by midday, after one man along the way had bought us three delicious cakes each. We've bought some wine and cheese for Mary's birthday party, and now we're sitting waiting for the boat which leaves in an hour. There are lots of hitchhikers heading home. Oh dear. Going home!

Tea With Milk
Folkestone, 26 August 1965

We begin to notice England as if it is another strange country. My diary:

> It's difficult to look right when you hitchhike or cross the road. And here's an English fish and chip shop, and people really are eating chips, wrapped in newspaper, with their fingers, in the street. You go into a café and you see everyone drinking tea, with milk in, so you have a cup. Tastes good. You understand everything that's being said around you but you are careful what you say because here you are easily understood. You don't have to speak French any more. It's raining of course. The people are reserved, and they stare. Gosh, the English really are like that. This was Folkestone to us because we'd become different during the holiday.

We went to Mary's auntie's house, an English semi. She welcomed us and gave us a cup of tea. The rooms were carpeted, wallpapered, clean and cosy, not like utility continental homes. We had bread and butter and a fry-up of eggs and bacon. The house smelled of furniture polish, fresh air, flowers, fresh-air spray, carpets and cooking. There was a spotless toilet that didn't make you shudder, and paper was provided. Afterwards there was hot water to wash in.

Later we went to the pub for a pint. You go in the bar, and everyone is talking about cricket. The atmosphere is smoky, warm and jovial. Mary was fascinated by the solidness of our money. I kept thinking of England as another country to be passed through on our travels. It really is amazing what you take for granted before you travel.

And what do the English make of us? Mary's Auntie Phil is a hairdresser. I had accidentally overheard her talking to a customer. "When you first see them, you'd think they were a pair of beatniks. But when you get talking to them you find they're really quite nice girls."

Next day, we head for Swindon, joining other hitchhikers who are moving around the country, many heading homewards. We pass two young Scotsmen hitching in their kilts. Pity they aren't going the same way as us. A long-distance lorry driver with rawhide looks picks us up, taking us almost as far as Swindon, and I spend much of the journey cooling his ardour with our African fan because it is so hot in the lorry.

Arab Women
Swindon, 27 August 1965

"Let's give my mother a real surprise," suggests Mary when we are at our destination. "Let's pretend we are Arabic women."

We have arrived two days before our deadline, at teatime in Swindon. I agree with Mary that this is an excellent idea, and we find a public toilet and dress up in our Moroccan *djellabas* and *yashmaks*. Carrying our palm-leaf donkey baskets filled with our fans, drums and teapots, we walk barefoot through the streets to Mary's house.

We knock on the door and Mary's mother opens it, gasps, not immediately realising who these apparitions are. She exclaims in horror: "You don't mean to say you walked through town like that!"

Our little escapade has backfired, and we are two abashed young ladies. Our joke had been intended to soften her anger for her daughter going to the desert without telling her in advance. But in a little while her kindly nature reasserts itself, and she warmly embraces her erring daughter and me. Now we must acclimatise to be being back in England: to having to wear shoes, to bearing in mind what the neighbours think, to speaking only English, and to eating tasteless food. We had left England on 5 July, crossed from France to Italy on 18 July, and on 27 July from Sicily to Tunis. Now it is 27 August. We have been immersed for seven weeks in cultures so entirely different from our own that this is going to be difficult.

I calculate in my diary that we have travelled 10,000 kilometres, or 6,500 miles, from the time we left England until we arrived in Boulogne. We have hitchhiked almost every kilometre of the way, our overnight accommodation has cost no more than the odd night in a youth hostel, and the food we've eaten had often been given to us by generous people along the way. We've learned about hospitality, true Islamic kindness and Spanish dancing, all of which will stay with us throughout our lives.

8

This Land Is Our Land

ENGLAND, SCOTLAND, WALES, IRELAND, AUTUMN 1965

WILD GROUP
SWINDON, 28–31 AUGUST 1965

We are in Swindon in time for Mary's twenty-first birthday as her mother truly wished. My diary:

> The house is topsy turvy with preparations for the party. There are about fifty people coming, and we're rather dreading the assortment of scruffs who we love best who'll be bound to come.
>
> When we went into town, I was turfed out of Long John's Kitchen because I was "pieds nus", barefoot. I'd been shoeless for days, and it was time to put it right, so I bought some red sandals.
>
> In the evening, some of us went to a house where there was folk-singing. It was very English and it's not easy to sing enthusiastically unless you like singing a solo.

Various of our friends find their way to Swindon. Two of the Irish boys I'd met at the *Fleadh* in Thurles, Len and Gar, have crossed the sea. Ralph, from our Tunisian encounter, all golden and clean now, has brought his friend Geoff from London. Jenny, Janet and Jean, our college friends, are here, and my brother Richard has come down from Newcastle.

"God designed you for better things than this," says a woman in a Swindon playground as we sing and drink and play on the children's slide and the witch's hat, and paddle in the freezing cold water of the pool. She is registering our grown-up-sized bodies and our childish behaviour, our smoking and our drinking.

Mary's parents are kindly and tolerant, but wary. On the actual day of her birthday her numerous relations and family friends assemble. This is an important event for her parents, she being older than her sisters and brother, Judith, John and Liz. Now Mary is twenty-one, old enough to have the key to the door and traditionally to marry without parental consent. Her parents must wonder if a future husband is among this wild-looking group.

Gar writes us a little ditty, which I glue in my diary. It starts with a toast to Mary and me on becoming 21, and then concludes:

We hope that they come to our lovely land
And we'll laugh and sing and just hold hands.
Or perhaps for the *Fleadh* they'll just come o'er
To jump and shout and see us once more.

Ralph, the tender-hearted Londoner, writes a seven-verse rhyme about a tramp who picked up other people's dropped cigarette ends to give them to people worse off than himself, before dying and being buried by the indifferent authorities. The first verse:

Nobody took notice of the old man in rags
As he stopped for the remnants of other folks' fags.

They passed him by without a word or a glance
And stared fixedly ahead as though in a trance.
Although I'm sure he saw them – every one,
And he's the one you might call a bum.

Hardly high-quality poetry; it justifies a hard-up travelling man, which he has at times been himself. These are boys who move along the roads, who travel with a light heart, who will sing a song or write a poem. Some of us pair up in gentle romances, lightly, learning about each other, but it doesn't last long.

My diary:

> Gradually over the days, people filtered away, Jenny and Janet to Ireland, Ralph, Geoff, Gar and Len to London, Jean to Bristol, the Welsh boy to Birmingham. Eventually Richard and I had to go home too and leave Mary all on her own. Everything was very sad. However, we have agreed to meet

again, at a Hitchhikers' Fleadh, on Friday 8 October, at the Black Lion in Hay-on-Wye.

The *Mappa Mundi* In Scotland
Loch Tay, 3 September 1965

Restlessness is in our bodies. We are used to the feeling of freedom on the open road. Once in Newcastle, I just can't stay still. I decide to make a journey to Scotland. This means heading north along the A1 and crossing the River Tweed on the seventeenth-century stone road bridge. On the *Mappa Mundi*, Berwick is a town of spires facing an island that could be Lindisfarne, shown as if it is just over the river from Newcastle. Edinburgh is a little further on, and is the town for which I am now heading. My diary:

> *I was looking around for other hitchers and met up with a French boy with long hair and baggy tartan trousers. One of his friends told me about the problems of Gaelic speakers. Before long I bumped into four lads from Glasgow, and a boy called Iain. We wandered around rather aimlessly and then I said, "Let's hitchhike to the Highlands." So we did. Iain and I went along by Loch Tay where we found an unlocked deserted farmhouse. There was still a little furniture in it with beds upstairs, and the electric lights worked. We wondered if an old man had died there, but there were no police or neighbours or ghosts so we stayed there, warm and comfortable, laughing a lot at ourselves sleeping in a ready-provided farmhouse by Loch Tay.*

Smutty City
Glasgow, 4–6 September 1965

Leaving Iain, I travel alone to Glasgow to visit my uncle and cousins. My diary:

I am in Uncle Jimmy's sitting room, lying on a divan bed dressed in pink pyjamas with some constructive modern jazz playing behind. Uncle Jimmy, the three wee laddies and Hammy the ragman are sleeping in the bedroom adjoining. So many diverse thoughts are going through my head, sleepy as I am. What a crazy few weeks it has been. How interesting people and their ideas are. How I hate belonging to a divided family, and how I am gradually getting used to it. How much I love music and songs. And I am a female torn between the desire to be a wife/mother type and an independent travelling woman. Another is that I'm dreading the thought of the work I must do at college. Although I don't do much about causing the panorama that ceaselessly revolves around me, I appreciate it all.

Take today in Glasgow. Grey drizzling streets, dashing raincoats, umbrellas, splashing buses, smutty air, gay shop windows. A jazz musician could do wonders with a scene like that, or an artist with a strong interpretive eye. Or an opposite situation this morning at Loch Tay. Iain and I got out of the farmhouse that we'd smuggled ourselves into, and went out into the clear rainwashed morning. The sun sparked on the loch, there were green brown hills, birds, cattle, flowers. You could imagine highland chieftains roaming around the glen, hear Scottish songs and music at every place name you see, feel the history and the ancientness of the mountains. A peaceful landscape disguising hard reality, a beautiful loch the result of a million dreary rainy days, highland chieftains and a million drops of splashed human blood; peaceful mountain sheep who endure endless snowy winters. It is easy to be deceived.

Uncle Jimmy and my youngest cousin Wee Stevie and I go to see Jimmy Logan in *Cupid Wore Skirts*, and I laugh more than I have for a long time. Why don't I ever do funny things, I wonder. I'm too serious. I drink whisky with my uncle, but decide I prefer tea.

From Glasgow, I hitchhike back to Newcastle across the Scottish Southern Uplands, through Lanark, Peebles and Selkirk, up the Clyde valley and down the Tweed. I pass through the woollen production towns, hearing in my mind the Irish Rovers singing that if it wasna for the weavers, we wadna have clothes made of wool. Here on the Scottish borders, workers are weaving behind the windows I can see on the tall stern riverside mills.

BIRTLEY ROUNDABOUT
NEWCASTLE, 8–13 SEPTEMBER 1965

Once back in Newcastle, I try to study a little at the local libraries. Soon it will be time to join Mary in North Wales. We are both realising that we must do some serious work if we are ever to qualify as teachers. Despite his hesitations at our method of transport, my father wants to be helpful, and he drives me as far as the roundabout at Birtley on the southern edge of the Tyneside conurbation. This is the classic starting point for people hitchhiking south. From there I get lifts to Sheffield and across the Peak District to Stockport. A lorry takes me to Nant Peris to meet Mary, near the foot of Snowdon. My diary:

> *My last lift was with a young Welsh lorry driver. Funny how easy it is to fall in love with lorry drivers. This makes my fourth. However as usual I discover that he is married.*

NORTH WALES
NANT PERIS, 14–17 SEPTEMBER 1965

Mary and I meet by the Vaynol Arms pub, and we find a farm where the kind woman agrees that we may sleep in the barn. We make a cosy bed for ourselves in the hay, and next day we hitch to Llanberis to the library so that Mary can make her maps. She is studying farming and landscape, making comparisons with the glaciated landscape here and in Chambon in France. My diary:

> It is pouring with rain as we leave Llanberis. We are soon drenched, and as usual lifts in rain are difficult. But the farmer's wife takes us in, we dry out a bit, and she makes us a huge supper of eggs, bread, butter, cheese and tea. Her husband gives us a cake and lets us sit by the table to write. The family are so kind that, while Mary writes up her maps and notes, I am motivated to write an essay in my diary about lovely Wales.
>
> "The Welsh appeal to me. They were here before the Romans and the Teutons, and they wouldn't be conquered. They were suppressed but never conquered. They live in the toughest most beautiful parts of Britain; they have marvellous traditions of music and a euphonic language, and the spirit of their lovely lands is carried across in their music.
>
> "Outside, the rain beats down, half of every lifetime, but the sunshine that will come makes the mountains look very lovely. In this land of beautiful sensitive reserved people, I always want to do something about my thumping self-satisfied English outlook on life. I want to go back to appreciating things the way the Welsh do, and help them preserve what they have because I don't think we can offer them anything better."

We sleep cosily in our bed of hay, and next day we trample up and down the valley, taking photos and drawing sketches of the U-shaped valley, the hanging waterfalls and Llyn Peris, the glacial lake separated from Llyn Padarn by the rushing waters of the Afon Arddu. We discover *roches moutonnées*, mounds of earth and rocks left by the glaciers, lying in sheep-shapes on the floor of the valley, as we'd seen in Chambon and where we'd learned the French word.

We have landed here on an important day. My diary:

The farmer told us that today here is "the day all the sheep are sold from this valley." It is the annual sheep sale of young breeding ewes and wether lambs which are the males. So that means drinking and making merry all day long. The farmers came down from the hills to Nant Peris. We peeped in at the sale. The auctioneer rattled away mostly in Welsh, but he came out with odd bits of English now and again. "Sseventy-ssix, sseventy-ssix, sseventy-seven and all guaranteed."

In the evening, we tidy ourselves up as well as we can and go to the Vaynol Arms. What we love more than anything else here in this damp, mountainous place is the singing. As we are near the mountains of Snowdon, there are always hikers and climbers with muddy boots coming to the pub. The Welsh customers like to sing, so there is one room of the pub for hikers and one for singers.

We sidle quietly into the singers' side and hope we will be accepted. They sing heartbreakingly beautifully, in easy harmony, mostly in Welsh, sometimes in English. Shyly, we join in the choruses when we can. We learn that some of the words of "Calon Lân" mean singing all through the day and all through the night. That's for us. It's what we love to do as we roam the countryside. The Welsh version of the song that we know as "Bread of Heaven" carries our spirits to the mountain peaks.

An old shepherd instructs us to go out and collect some rushes. He weaves them into a rattle and puts a couple of stones inside. We shake it in time with the music as we sing. Later, settling into our beds in the hay while the tunes and words and harmonies are still echoing in our minds, we hear the boy hikers come to sleep in the cowshed next door.

The singing isn't yet over for us. We have made friends with the Jones family, who live in Llanberis. They have invited us to their house, and next day, while their mother feeds us amply, her three young sons sing more hymns and songs in harmony for us. Then they drive us to the A5, where we can get easy lifts south. We must leave our hearts in Wales for the present.

To Cornwall
Dartmoor, 18 September 1965

Cornwall is our destination. I must do the field research for my geography special study. Lifts are easy enough, and towards the end of the day we arrive in the county of Devon. My diary:

> We knew we'd have to spend the night somewhere along the way, and we suddenly remembered that our college friend Di Bray lives in Exmouth. Oh well, we say to each other, we'll pop in and spend the night at Di's. We hadn't bargained on her mother though.
>
> "She isn't in," she said briefly, probably thinking something like "these scruffy beatniks aren't getting anywhere with me. What a disgrace, turning up like that." She went on: "I don't know when Diane will be back. Maybe not at all tonight. She's visiting a friend." Probably she was thinking they won't wait now and I'm not going to ask them in.
>
> We thought to ourselves that it's nice to know we don't have to spend a night here after all, and we felt sorry for her stingy respectable life, and for Di who's lived with her for 21 years.
>
> So we hitched further towards Dartmoor and knocked on the door of a farmhouse. They gave us a bed in the hayshed, and the lovely Devonshire farmer's wife cooked up our food for us on her stove. She was as pretty as peaches

and cream, and her husband sparkled with fun. We learned all about their rights to graze animals on Dartmoor Forest and the seasonal round-ups. They were kind and unpretentious, and had no need to be like Di's mum, we felt, because they are secure in their love and their work. We had a chilly but exciting night in the barn as there were plenty of mice and rats running around. Next morning, we were wakened and given an excellent breakfast before we were sent on our way.

Lilies Of The Field
St Cleer, 18 September 1965

While we hitchhike the last few miles to Cornwall, we are thinking that we may need a rest. My diary:

Since 5 July, we've been on the move practically non-stop, with a few days' rest at home each. Our minds are attuned to hitching, travelling; we do it expertly and automatically. But we've had so many crazy experiences, seen so many fantastic people and places, that it all needs time to settle in. We're developing a lollopy turn-and-hitch walk, have highly stereotyped conversations with drivers, and I've been getting a lot of car sickness lately. It's time we had a rest. And we'll be getting it soon. Once the Cornwall work is done, it will be Hereford Teacher Training College until Christmas. We'll have to become young ladies again.

Yet we are full of optimism. My diary:

Lots of people smiled back at us today: a Spanish middle-aged married man who's been here since 1940 and was delighted to meet us because we could speak a little of his language, a crippled old man, people in cars, a man trimming a sports field on a tractor. When people smile because they can see we're happy, that's good all round.

I am expecting that I will find a friendly farmer whose lifestyle and farming methods I can compare with that of the Berthelot family in Brittany. Like Mary's farm family in Nant Peris, someone is sure to welcome us. We head for the village of St Cleer, on the edge of Bodmin Moor.

"Philip is certainly not allowed to travel around like you girls do," states the pub owner in St Cleer, as we chat over half a pint of cider soon after our arrival. We have met his son, who is intrigued by our sudden appearance in his village. He is sixteen years old, with a tentative smiling face and locks of brown hair hanging over his forehead.

Our first action is to find where we can spend the night, and we approach Tremabe Farm. The neat granite farmhouse faces directly on to the road going through the village, and it has tidy clusters of buildings behind including a barn. My diary:

When we knocked on the door, the man and woman, Mr and Mrs Couch, laughed their heads off, and said, yes, we could sleep in the barn. Later, they took us in, gave us a lovely supper, and to crown our joys presented us with a beautiful double bed. We feel so lucky. A woman today had said to us, "Better to be born lucky than rich."

It is Harvest Festival evening, and Mary and I go to join the service in the village church. My diary:

This is quite new for me, to go to a Church of England service. Mary sang all the prayers and psalms, and I sang the hymns. It was mostly old people there, but they certainly sang out.

> The vicar spoke clearly about modern man who has lost his humility and become all mixed up with mechanical things and his own cleverness. Then he read out of the Bible:

> "Lay not up for yourselves treasures upon earth, where moth and rust doth corrupt, and where thieves break through and steal. For where your treasure is, there will your heart be also.
> "And why take ye thought for raiment? Consider the lilies of the field, how they grow. They toil not, neither do they spin. And yet I say unto you, that even Solomon in all his glory was not arrayed like one of these."

I find a copy of the Bible later and copy this selection down in my diary in red. We liked the message because it allies with our philosophy of hitchhiking: to have few possessions but lots of trust, and to spread smiles and happiness.

It tallies with the fashionable Beatles song where they sing that money can't buy them love. Of course it can't. We know that. It can't buy us love either, oh, no, no.

Celtic Land
St Cleer, 19 September 1965

St Cleer parish spreads up to Bodmin Moor. The landscape and the Tremabe Farm bountifully provide me with materials of interest and comparison with Saint-Gilles-Pligeaux in Britanny. There are granite tors and megalithic monuments for geology and prehistory. The medieval church spires in both places stand out in the low surrounding hills, and they each have holy wells commemorating Celtic saints. I check both farms' crop rotation and yearly cycles of planting and harvesting. The Cornish farmer uses tractors rather than horse-power, but both have a few cows, sheep, pigs and poultry. St Cleer is a more mechanised, modern farm, but I enjoy working out the differences. The most significant is the layout of the fields. In Brittany, M. Berthelot's farm is split up into tiny, scattered fields, and has an almost medieval element of self-sufficiency. It is yet to be subjected to President de Gaulle's scheme of *Remembrement* or consolidation of holdings. By comparison, Tremabe Farm is nicely compacted.

One of my most interesting discoveries is a written Cornish version of the Lord's prayer, "Our Father Who Art in Heaven". I can compare it with the Breton version I collected in Saint-Gilles-Pligeaux. Although the languages are very different, a few phrases like "our daily bread" are similar, for example *bara pem dezick* in Breton and *bara pup detholl* in Cornish.

While Mary hitchhikes off to meet Jean Ives, a French boyfriend, in St Just, I set about my work, measuring, making draft maps, taking photographs, and becoming more friendly with Philip. Field work is always more enjoyable in company with an attractive young man. When the time comes to leave, Philip reassures us he'll find his own way to hitchhike to Hereford despite his father's restrictions.

Back To Base
Hereford, 24 September 1965

Mary and I have sung our way back to Hereford for the start of the autumn term of our final year. Since returning from North Africa, we must settle down after the summer's activities. At the same time, our college in Hereford is becoming a focal point between London and Ireland. My diary:

> *Now we're back in college. I'm sitting here in my blue room about 2 am after having heard everyone's tales. Jenny and Janet are just back from Ireland, Chris from Yugoslavia, Margaret and Val from Greece, Tonie and Val from tours round the Welsh agricultural shows. It feels great to be really clean again, and I can bear the thought of laying down that*

rucksack for a while. Tonight I was on the phone to Ralph in London. Then Len phoned from London too and he's coming up tomorrow on his way back to Ireland. Gerry is now working in Germany.

All my belongings are cluttered around the room, the Moroccan tom-tom drum, the guitar, last year's sombrero, the French wooden sabots, the tiny Dutch clogs, the palm leaf donkey basket from the desert, my new black shoes from Newcastle. Everything of past times. Now there's the prospect of nine months' hard work ahead, and the inviting date of July 5th 1966 awaiting, when we will travel away from Hereford for the last time.

I make a colourful map in my diary showing England, Wales and Scotland, France, Italy and North Africa, and back again through France. It shows all the routes Mary and I have travelled between 5 July and 24 September. I calculate a total of 8,500 miles. Virtually all of this has been by putting out our thumbs, smiling sweetly and being offered lifts. We have so little money and yet such exciting lives. We are finding our way round our own country as well as exotic overseas places. Northumberland, Glasgow, the Scottish borders, North Wales, Cornwall.

Along the roads, our eyes have looked into those of many charming young men, and we've wondered, dreamed, rejected and sometimes lingered. Len turns up on 30 September, and he and Jenny are now forming an attachment. Mary is linked with Chris, a university student in London. I am fond of Philip from Cornwall. Tonie is still in love with her lorry driver boyfriend, Ivor, and Val has a strong relationship with Denis in North Wales.

But now we must seriously start working or we'll never end up as respectable teachers in front of a class of children. I am told by the vice principal, Miss Bookham, that I should try to look and behave like a third-year student. I read Camus's *The Fall*, Oscar Wilde's *Picture of*

Dorian Gray and Walt Whitman's poetry, and play my tin whistle. We are obliged to hand in essays and devise psychology experiments. Tonie and Jenny must prepare their plays, Mary and I make maps, Chris and Mary create dancing routines. A sense of finality is hitting us. We must take life more seriously. But not too seriously. Our hitchhikers' *Fleadh* in Hay-on-Wye is only a couple of weeks away.

Tonie, Mary and I often attend Hereford folk music club, which has a mixture of people who like to sing the old-fashioned English country songs like "Green Grow the Rushes-oh" and those who follow currently fashionable folksingers like Woody Guthrie, Joan Baez and of course Bob Dylan. We lean towards the latter.

We have our own speciality, me having picked up various songs from Tyneside including "Keep Your Feet Still Geordie Hinny" and "Blaydon Races". As for "Cushie Butterfield", we can certainly sing about this big, bonnie lass who undoubtedly likes her beer. My diary:

> *Tonie, Mary and I made our début at the folk club singing Tyneside songs. We weren't so very marvellous but they liked it and asked us to sing next week.*

Fairies In The Forest
Delamere Forest, 2 October 1965

It is the straightforward masculinity of lorry drivers that appeals. Like us, they are always on the move. When we climb into their cabs, we reward them with our cheerful conversation, which helps pass the time on long and often repetitive journeys. Ivor the Driver, as Tonie calls her boyfriend, lives in North Wales; she and I make a plan visit him at his home. I can combine this with a meeting with my sister Rosie at Delamere Forest. My diary:

> *Tonie and I gleefully departed on Friday night for north Wales. We met Ivor in Wrexham and then went to a Welsh*

pub, The Farmers, in Trueddyn. There I enjoyed myself in my customary way by learning some Welsh and by asking the old farmers to sing Welsh songs. Later on, at Ivor's house, we listened to Welsh songs with his mother on their record player.

His family cottage is cosy and homely. They are Welsh people who speak the language and care for their tradition. Everything in the house was flowery, the curtains, carpets, chair covers, Mrs Jones' dresses, tablecloths.

Next day Ivor and Tonie drove me to Delamere where we waited to meet Rosie. I sat in the forest playing my pipe. This is a real old English forest, filled with dreams of Robin Hood and Merrie England. When you walk on the road between the ancient trees, and there's a path of sky overhead, you feel you could easily fly up there, and out into the open expanse of airiness.

But try and explain that to Ivor! He's so practical! He just didn't understand. He kept teasing us about playing aeroplanes, which is quite off the point. As Tonie said: "It's about as deflating as people who don't believe that an elf or a goblin or a fairy queen can live inside a rosebud."

The roads have led us to him, and now lead us away.

Hitchhikers' Fleadh
Hay-on-Wye, 8–10 October 1965

It is time for our hitchhikers' *Fleadh*. From Hereford, we have sent messages to our network of friends in Newcastle upon Tyne, London, Birmingham and Ireland to meet at the Black Lion pub in the little town of Hay-on-Wye on 8 October. Mr Beattie, the owner, is a Scotsman who christened his two children Elspeth and Ian, and he has a genial reputation. We feel that we might be welcomed there. We have little money and not much food, and no planned accommodation. This will be our own version of the *Fleadh* in Ireland.

"We're the only ones here," Jenny says to me, as we look around the interior of the Black Lion, until she notices two rucksacks. Ralph with his friend Steve from London roll in through the door. Now there are four of us, and we'll have to wait awhile to see who else turns up as there is no way to find out. We soon become friendly with the Hay boys from the Black Lion darts team, Flash Keylock, Ian Beattie, Des Price. My diary:

They drove us to a dance in Gladestry. It was a local hop, and we enjoyed it until someone stole my shoes and Jenny's hat. It was the Kingston boys, traditional enemies of the Hay boys. We pulled our lads away to prevent a fight. However Jenny remained hatless and me shoeless. Back to Hay we went, and by 2 am we four were wandering around with our bags by the castle looking for somewhere to sleep. I remembered that there was a barn on the fields behind the castle, and there it was. Empty of straw but enclosed and wind-free.

Next day we sat by the lovely River Wye and waited to see who would turn up. A girl going pony trekking called Yvonne joined us, and Jean and Janet from Hereford. Then as we sat in the sun watching Hay bridge, along came a great gang

of scruffy hitchers, Rosie and Alicia from the north, Ralph, Len and his friends Gar and Leo from Ireland, all with sleeping bags and guitar. A little later along came Brian from Birmingham, Nino and Garnet from Hereford, Geoff from London, Philip from Cornwall, Dick the Ban the Bomber.

I find time to visit my friend Christine and her small baby. She had been my best friend when we were children but, whereas her life is here, mine has taken an outer direction. Part of me would like to live as she does, in the streets that wind up and down, among the familiar faces from my childhood.

"The faces are always the same, just as they were as infants," Ralph comments. I wander into the Wye Café, where in my teens I'd served teas and mopped the floor while listening to the juke box. I scout around nostalgically leaving the others in the pub for a while. I cross the bridge, and from the hill on the Clyro road I look across the rooftops of the town and the castle chimneys. In the background is the mountain I can see from the window of my blue room at college. It seems to magnetise me.

The Black Lion is our hostelry again that evening. We drink and sing and drink some more. My diary:

Everyone was happy. Jenny said, "You know the trouble is, Bridge, everyone just loves everyone else too much."

I was talking to the Hay lads and Rosie with the Warners, gypsies who spoke little bits of Romany with her, and who invited her to their camp.

When we eventually left the pub, we all rolled along to the barn, but someone had locked us out. There was one side area with an open wall where we made do, but it was much colder, being a bit late in the year for this wild behaviour. A bright full moon shone into our dark wooden barn.

The farmer came along in the morning. He bade us good-day and was quite friendly so we gave him a Guinness.

Even though it was Sunday morning, the boys wanted to go back to drinking again, but we girls didn't. Rosie wanted to go to the gypsy camp but Alicia insisted that it was a long hitchhiking journey back to Newcastle so they left. I was sad to see my little sister go.

Jenny and I went to the Warners' camp on Sheephouse Farm. Cecil was sitting by the campfire, his head hanging heavy after last night at the Black Lion. He's a handsome, active gypsy. Two little dogs nose around, and a three-year-old lad keeps peeping at us. Cecil's wife Betty comes out, smiling at us in a friendly manner. She gives us tea and then says she'll do "the hobbins". A big iron hook dangles over the fire on which she hangs a frying pan. We cook eggs and sausages and eat with bread and no knives and forks, real gypsy fashion. We decide to help her, so Jenny and I pump water, and as Jenny is tall she reaches up to clean the caravan windows. We help Betty shake her mats. Then we sit by the sweet-smelling wood fire, talking in the sunshine. This is a fantastic life, we're both thinking, and how we'd like to marry handsome gypsies and travel around the country.

Betty shows us old photos with the ancient wagons and gypsy clothes. "It's an 'ealthy life out here, not like a hordinary 'ouse." We promise to return and invite them to visit us in Hereford.

Sheephouse Farm is famous for its pedigree Hereford cattle, which I greatly admire. We go to look at them, and Jenny loves the bulls as much as I do. It is a perfect day. We wander back to Hay, where the boys are waiting, still sitting over their pints in the Black Lion. My diary:

We trek out of the pub, along the streets of Hay. Everyone loves the little town. "It reeks with incest," says Steve knowingly. "It's gotta crazy character," says Ralph.

In my diary, I write that I think the Hay people have enjoyed having us. Perhaps they did. Hay is a small, rather ordinary town, and we have been an unusual set of visitors.

Not ready to end our time together, we decide to move to Michaelchurch Escley, a few miles south of Hay, and in England. My diary:

> Jenny and I were hilarious, singing as we walked along in the wind under the blue sky. We played the mouth organ, and then the church organ to accompany ourselves singing "All Things Bright and Beautiful". We discussed our Ideal Community, which is to be based on Love, Understanding, Tolerance and Unselfishness. And our Practical Community is almost the same except that people come and go instead of being together in one place.
>
> We sat in the pub by the warm fire waiting for the others. The farmers and hunters were all talking in different accents from deep Herefordshire brogue to destructive county English. Gradually others arrived, and we livened up the pub by dancing, singing and drinking. They didn't seem to mind.
>
> Afterwards we all found overnight accommodation in an abandoned water mill by the Escley stream. The mill was filled with hay, cosy and warm, and everyone was very happy.

Our little *Fleadh* must end. Next day, some of the boys hitchhike back homeward while we smuggle the others into our girls-only hostel, past the signing-in book, subduing wild, noisy behaviour until the morning.

AMERICAN JAZZ
BIRMINGHAM, 22 OCTOBER 1965

Jenny and I have hitchhiked on a Friday evening, through the fog, to Birmingham Town Hall. It is the National Jazz Federation's 4th American Folk Blues Festival. We have tickets number 27 and 28 in the orchestra gallery, the cheapest five-shilling seats. Hereford has a jazz club, and we are regular attenders, but this is the real thing. My diary:

> We loved the long loose-limbed black singers and we looked at the mostly students in the audience along with us, and pondered of the nature of Man. The performers were so relaxed and could they sing! There was a huge fat woman singer, Big Mama Thornton, and Sonny Boy Williamson, a tall lanky man with his harmonica.
>
> Hitching back, we accepted a lift with four boys in one vehicle, going down the motorway. They were impolite and aggressive. By the time we got out and away we resolved never again to get in a lift where we would be outnumbered.

DANCE AND DAFT
HEREFORD, 23 OCTOBER 1965

Our college is sufficiently relaxed to organise a Tramps and Vamps dance. We are quite surprised that they would allow a theme about roadside wanderers, the tramps presumably the boys and the vamps the girls. Tickets are three shillings at the door. Jenny and I enlist an international group from around Hereford, three Pakistanis, two Nigerians, two Italians, some students from the Art College and a collection of other neighbourhood boys. My diary:

> Jenny and I were hectically dancing around everywhere when suddenly Jean and Alphonso announced they were engaged. I hopped around for about ten minutes. At the end, I was so exhausted I slept in a sleeping bag in Jenny's room because it was impossible to waddle through the mess of people in my room.
>
> As we had a geography exam on Monday, it was strictly necessary for me to work all day on Sunday. In effect I did a few hours' general time wasting in between falling asleep over my books. So that is why I feel quite sure, along with several others, Mary, Tonie and Val, that my chance of anything but a D pass is negligible.
>
> This week we have been working, that is in between late nights, nights out, afternoons shopping, and afternoon snoozes. I wouldn't mind working if I could ever get round to doing it, but there never seems to be much time.
>
> Today, Miss Bradley the dance lecturer said to me, "Do you really have to have all that stuff hanging round your neck Bridget?" I only had my parachute medal from Toni, my knot of wood and an Irish leprechaun.
>
> Jenny tipped a bottle of water over a girl as she came up the stairs. The girl wasn't amused. We never seem to grow up.
>
> I finished reading Alan Paton's Debbie, Go Home. This racial intolerance is unknown to me. Next I'm going to read Bertrand Russell's Satan in the Suburbs.

Cold Night
Clun, 12–13 November 1965

"We need the peace of the mountains," says Jenny. My diary:

> *We hitchhiked northwards until we reached the cool green valleys of the Shropshire border with Wales where we could see snow on the mountains. Suddenly we'd travelled from summer into winter. In the church in Clun, we played the organ and my tin whistle. The vicar came in, and he warned us that we'd have a cold night in the youth hostel. This we did, along with a gang of Londoners. The hostel is an old water mill with grinding stones and wheels still intact.*

Clun is in England, and I encourage Jenny to go Wales. A family with three little boys take us to Newcastle-on-Clun, where they invite us to their cottage on a grassy bank with chickens pecking about. They give us tea, and show us their very old Welsh dresser. We are near the border. Once we pass the *Croeso i Gymru* road sign, Welcome to Wales, I tell Jenny I can feel a different atmosphere.

"That's nonsense, Bridget," she says. When I insist, she says that the fields and the hills can't be so different just because we've crossed an invisible line on a map. I can't deny this, but I am filled with a sense of romanticism, the pull of the west, of the hills, a sense of drama, of the mystery of the language I can't understand. My diary:

> *Our next lift was a friendly farmer who told us about his farm, his life, and advised us to be very wary of men. He must have anticipated our next lift, which was with a nuisance of a man, and we were glad to get out of his car. We passed on to Llangurig, and down the Wye valley, as beautiful and irreproachably lovely as the music of Wales. Our next lift was with an American Baptist preacher, a blind believer. The last*

lift was with a man who brought us through Rhayader to the doors of our college. He told us he was experimenting growing fruit trees at eight hundred feet in the Brecon Beacons.

We are back at the centre once again. We've been off, out, around, through the hills, down the Wye valley and are now in Hereford with our view looking west into Wales.

A Mouse
Hereford, 20 November 1965

I feel I need company in my blue room. My diary:

> Today I bought a mouse from the pet shop in Hereford. She's a beautiful little grey, pink-eyed thing.

I have created a nest box for her out of a wooden crate that had held oranges. It is open at the front, but it has a two-inch shelf that she can look over. I've put one of my black wooden clogs from France in the crate, filled it with hay, and there she is making a cosy nest for herself. She is free to climb out of her box onto the windowsill, and up the curtains, if she wants to, but most of the time she seems to be happy in her nest. Later, my diary:

> My mouse is becoming very tame. She enjoys running around on the grass when I take her outside, and she also exercises herself on the windowsill. She seems to like hiding from me. Yesterday she hid in the bed. Tonight she was sitting on the curtain rail.

ESSENTIAL EXAM
HEREFORD, 21 NOVEMBER 1965

My diary:

Our full and firm intentions are to swot hard for the History of Education exam all week. But there are always so many other things to do. Tuesday evening was the Dance Group's show for their assessment. Mary did the introductions, and along with Chris and the other students, they leapt and performed spectacularly. When I got back, I fell straight to sleep, but Philip rang to announce he was in Hereford. This is ten o'clock at night. He arrived at the hostel door, so I immediately got a late key and whisked out with him into town where we had conversations with a brother and sister hot-dog-sellers. I left him sleeping in the deserted house by the station, freezing cold, and in the morning he came up to college where we smuggled him some breakfast. Then we went to the market to see the animals being sold, and on to the Cathedral. The sun shone in through the clerestory windows making the stone glow pink. The organ began playing Bach, then some other wild music, then quiet music. He had to leave at midday, and I felt sad.

In the afternoon, Jenny and I cycled into town to see our Pakistani friends, and they spoke to us about racial prejudice and Islam.

Poor Mary had to go to see Miss Hipwell on Wednesday. She hasn't to work on the post at Christmas because she is getting bad marks, particularly from Mr Tidswell, so she must apply herself to her studies from now on.

That's the trouble. There are so many interesting things to do that there isn't much time for studying. We had the exam, but none of us feel we did very well.

Winter Gathering
Crickhowell, 2–7 December 1965

At our next hitchhikers' *Fleadh* we arrange with our enlarging network of friends to meet in Crickhowell thirty or so miles south-west of Hereford in the valley of the Usk. Boyfriends and girlfriends appear from all directions. On Thursday night, Ralph and Geoff arrive in Hereford and, during Friday, Len and Leo from Dublin and my sister Rosie from Newcastle. We hitchhike off to Crickhowell, taking the A465 south-westward into Wales. This time, Philip manages to come from Cornwall and is waiting for us at the Bear. That makes eight of us, and I feel that these are eight of the best people in the world. Not everyone agrees. My diary:

We had a row with the repulsive pseudo-aristocratic pub owner, and there was nearly a fight as his fat powdered wife grabbed Ralph's hair, and made a derogatory remark on the lines of – you can't tell the men from the girls –

and – the best thing about you boys is your women. This attracted the local boys who arrived to join in the fun. The local policeman came and quietened things down. He was mainly on our side.

Later, we wandered up the mountain seeking a barn. Jenny and Len got lost, and the rest of us slept in a horse box, dry but rather cold. In the morning we crept away as the sun rose and made pink clouds in the valley over Crickhowell. Steve turned up from Birmingham in the morning. I am beginning to get tired of spending all day in pubs, and drag people off for walks whenever I can. In the evening Garnet turned up from Hereford, bringing Mary, Jean and Janet in his car, and Rossie and Lorna hitched here. We made our way to the nearby hamlet of Llangattock where there is a singing pub. There we sang to our hearts' content, joining in with the local people, and offering our own Irish and Geordie songs from time to time.

Over the next couple of days, we all need to work our various ways home, along the roads north, south, east and west. By Tuesday evening, Leo and Len are setting off on the train from Hereford towards Holyhead and the boat to Ireland. The threads are broken. Mary, Jenny and I are on Hereford station, waving, alone, everyone gone.

Mary Sews Her Dress
Hereford, 13–15 December 1965

It is time for the college's formal dance, and Mary's boyfriend, Chris, comes from London to escort her. She wears a full-length silky dress that she stitched by hand herself, and he is smart in a suit.

These are end-of-term activities. The college music students perform the Christmas Oratorio and the second-year drama students produce Molière's *The Intellectual Ladies*. The programme states that it is "not inappropriate to present this play in a college devoted to the Education of Women".

The last day of term arrives. My diary:

> *This term has whizzed by. It's been the most exciting since I came to college. Not a minute's been spare, met many marvellous people, new exciting lecturers, more interesting work, and we ourselves really have worked. We were busy up to the last minute, Jenny writing up her philosophy essay, and Mary her drama one.*

COAL PITS
CUMBERLAND, 16 DECEMBER 1965

We must move on. My diary:

> *Pack a bag, put mouse in pocket, tidy the room, and set out for the North. Keep hitching, and in three lifts arrive in a remote corner of Cumberland the same night to meet my sister Rosie.*

This is yet another new part of the country for me. I have crossed the Lake District, passing Windermere, Rydal Water, Derwentwater and Bassenthwaite, and over the mountains beyond. Rosie and her friend take me to a dance, where I discover that lots of the local lads are coal miners. As we leave the area next day, looking across the Solway to Scotland, we see several derelict local pits and small pit villages, all part of the West Cumberland coalfield. Soon we're home, back in Canny Newcassel, with my father and brother in one house and mother and younger brother in another. This hurts us all but must be dealt with. Christmas passes, and I am given a present of a new tin whistle and a book of Scottish songs. My father gives me a record of the song "The Lambton Worm", a Geordie version of the St George and Dragon myth. That's one I can practise for Hereford folk club. I try to apply myself, and work on essays about Freud and Eysenck. At last, I am becoming a conscientious student. But I can't work too hard. Ireland beckons.

Winter Road
To Dublin, 27–29 December 1965

"I want to come too," says my younger brother Stephen, who is thirteen years old. As we discuss this, Richard, who is fifteen, says that he'd like to come, and seventeen-year-old Rosie is taking it for granted that she and I will go together to Ireland for the New Year. I warn them of the cold and uncertainties ahead, but they are not to be dissuaded. We decide to go and pack our bags quickly. At 4 pm, we are ready. Our father is looking at us gloomily. He doesn't seem to have the energy to argue with us. Suddenly, and uncharacteristically, he offers to drive us as far as Gretna Green. This is well beyond Carlisle, and a helpful start along the way to Stranraer in the south-west of Scotland. My father enables us to have a realistic chance of reaching Stranraer in time for the morning boat to Northern Ireland. My diary:

> *From Gretna, we split up, Rosie with Stephen and Richard with me. We agreed to meet in Stranraer at the ticket office. It was a beautiful starlit night, crystal clear, ice cold, freezing freezing cold. Lifts were short and far between. In between them, we gazed at the frosty, starlit fields and romantic tree outlines while our toes became frozen and our noses glowed blue. From 11 pm to 2.30 am we walked around the whole twelve miles of Wigtown Bay, lights gleaming on the coast, sea smells floating up in sharp-nipping air, starlight reflected in the still waters. Eventually, aching to the bone, feeling we could neither go on nor stop, a Land Rover picked us up, and we arrived at*

Stranraer at 4 am where we met the others. For a couple of hours we managed to get some sleep before the boat left at 7 am. We followed the rocky coastline of Scotland towards the white snowy cliffs of Ireland, watching a sunrise behind us.

Once in Ireland, separating again into couples, we circle the roads around Belfast before heading south to Dublin.
Our sixpenny road maps show us the way. There are more icy walks among frosted scenes, with fairy-white trees and black cattle. In a mini-van, we have a near-accident when the vehicle spins round and round on the icy surface before crashing into a wall with a bang. None of us suffers more than a scare. Richard and I manage to arrive in Dublin in the evening and meet up with Rosie and Stephen, as cold and hungry as us. The youth hostel is a cheerless place. We are too tired to complain. Wearing all our clothes, we lie

under the grey woollen blankets, heavy with damp, on the cold, iron-framed bunk beds.

Hospitality
Dublin, 30 December 1965

Our Irish friends are expecting us in a general sort of way, not being quite sure who will turn up, or when. We take a bus to Drimnagh on the outskirts of the city. Once we have found our friend Gar's house, and woken him out of his bed, we are soon playing our tin whistles and guitar. There is a knock on the door. Jenny has managed to get here with Geoff from London and his friend Paddy. At night we all go to the famous Slattery's pub, with our Irish friends Leo, June, Paddy and Len. Truly we are in the real Ireland again. My diary:

> *No-one knew where we were going to spend the night. We certainly didn't want to go to that ghastly youth hostel in Dublin again. We said we'd find a barn and all go together, Jenny, me and my brothers and sister, Geoff who only had sevenpence, and Paddy. In the end, we didn't. June took in Rosie, Jenny and me. Len took Geoff and Paddy, and Leo took Richard and Stephen.*

This is the thing about being in Ireland. People are helpful and hospitable, and don't make a fuss. The next day, we all get up late and chat with June's mother. I like the easy-going Irish outlook on life, happy-go-lucky without being irresponsible, and laughing at class distinction.

The charm is in the music. Both this night, of 30 December, and the next, New Year's Eve, we go to pubs. My little brothers are getting their first experiences of the singing and laughter of Ireland, accompanied of course by the drinking. At O'Donaghue's, there is ballad singing and Irish bagpipe playing. A man playing the tin whistle is very encouraging to me, the enthusiastic learner. Nothing compares though with the music on New Year's Night when we all pile off to see Ronnie Drew and the Dubliners. My diary:

> We were all in one huge room with the Dubliners there against the wall. We sat right by the front and could hear beautifully. These brilliant musicians sang Irish songs I know and don't know: Ragman's Ball, The Rocky Road to Dublin, Tramps and Hawkers, and played a lovely Irish tune called Mise Éire on the mandolin. Everyone sings, joins in, and there was no rowdyism or bawdiness at all.
>
> Our heads were full of tunes and music as we walked back in the cold windy night, all the way to Drimnagh from Dublin, by the side of the Liffy River lit up like Paris.

Chocolates Too
Dublin, 31 December 1965

I hadn't really known that our rambunctious freedom-loving male friends from Dublin would expect to take us to a formal dance.

Jenny has come prepared with a long blue dress for this event, to which Len has invited her. I feel a bit left out of the equation, although Leo offers in a gentlemanly fashion to escort me. But I have only my denim skirt and hitchhiking clothes, so what shall I do?

"See what I have that will fit you," offers Annette. I choose a slim-line grey dress with yellow and red flowers, pretty although a bit too tight. Len arrives and presents Jenny with a huge box of chocolates, this being apparently the Irish custom. It signifies something a bit extra-special. Both he and Leo are on their best behaviour and look smart in their dark suits, ties, white shirts and waistcoats. Jenny and I are learning that this is how the Irish court their girlfriends. We eat and dance and drink at the formal dance, and time flies by until we leave, exhausted, at 4 am to return to our kindly host families.

To The Ferry
Larne to Newcastle, 2–4 January 1966

Sometimes hitchhiking is dreamily easy. Certainly this can be so in warm weather, in good light and on sunny days. We are now learning how bad it can be in the opposite conditions.

Leo's brother Ernie gives us a good start by driving north thirty miles out of Dublin as far as Drogheda. After that it becomes very difficult. Once again, I am with my brother Richard and Rosie with Stephen. My diary:

We stood, we froze, we walked, we got soaked in rainstorms, we shivered and generally hated every minute of it. At long last, a man took us in a car to his house and gave us some supper. This was near Larne, the departure harbour for Stranraer. It was 10.30 at night and we had a grand total of five shillings plus our boat fare. Then he took us to a guest house in Larne where he left us for the night. Richard and I were shown into a room with a double bed. I'm ashamed to say that we walked out without paying the next morning as we didn't have enough money to pay. But we're going to post them some money. We eventually met Rosie and Stephen who had slept the night in the ferry boat waiting room.

The crossing was beautiful, the sea as calm as a lake with the cliffs of Ireland behind, small islands dotted in the sea, the sun shining warm and low. Before long we could see the rocky coastline of Scotland ahead, and we were in the sea between the two countries.

Hitching home was absolutely dreadful. I was with Stephen. We left the boat in high spirits only to have the same as before, wait, freeze, walk, get hungry, freeze freeze freeze. It took us until 7.30 pm to get to Brampton, between Carlisle and Newcastle. We had just enough money to pay for the bus, so we decided to do this, and arrived home at 10.30 pm.

We expected Philip from Cornwall, and he arrived next day, having hitched from Torquay overnight, then ended up on trains and buses on which he kept sleeping past all the stops. Now he's sleeping on the settee in the front room.

Jenny rang. She and Geoff and Paddy had had a terrible time hitching back to London too, but like us, they soon recovered. As I write this, we are all feeling contented, and Rosie is in the kitchen making us scrambled egg.

New Year
Hereford, 28 January 1966

I find that all my friends seem to be applying for jobs after they qualify. Except me. I'm uncertain. Mary and I discuss Voluntary Service Overseas. This might be a compromise between my urgent desire to travel and the need to be responsible.

Mild weather causes me to rhapsodise. My diary:

Outside the blackbird is really singing again. Even Mouse smells the earthy rainy air when I open the west-facing window and scents this new feeling she's never had before. Grey squirrels play on the tree outside, and those singing golden daffodils in my room lighten my heart every time I come in. It's five o'clock and it isn't even dark, and soon I'm going hitchhiking again to see Phil. And right now, I'm scribbling along and loving everything I'm seeing and hearing, and loving the thought of being with Phil tomorrow, by the sea in South Devon, loving all those girls I can hear chatting in the corridor, the dog whose bark comes in clearly from outside, Jenny working on her history essays, loving little Mouse as she's hiding in my coat now, loving having the windows open because it's not too cold, loving everyone up in Newcastle – hope it's not still cold there – loving the Wales feeling coming over in the wind from the Black Mountains on the skyline, loving the new buds on the trees only just daring to open in case this spring is a false alarm. I'm even loving Mr Bennett the psychology lecturer, who's my ideal of strength and intelligence, loving that crow going Craa Craa Craa outside, loving being me in every way, loving that road stretching away ahead tonight, especially loving those three daffodils beside me now, laughing oh quietly, so happily. I can hear Mouse chewing my coat. Well, she's welcome. I must go and get packed. Away I'm going again, tin whistle and all.

SOUTH-WESTERLY
TORQUAY, 29 JANUARY 1966

My friend Jean and I hitch together as far as Bristol, and we arrive there in three lifts. My diary:

Jean and I left on the dot of 6 am. We started along the Ross road, and got to Bristol in three hours ten minutes flat, in three lifts.

The first was with two yobbish boys who had nothing else to do so they drove us to Ross. They stopped for a drink. Jean was dubious but I acted as if I didn't understand their intentions. They didn't talk much, but in the end they let us out like lambs at Ross.

Next lift, a fantastic man, another of my Ideal Types. Brawn and Brains combined. He was an international long-distance lorry driver, rare enough in our experience. He told us about his trips to Paris and back four times a week, his trips to Greece, Sicily – he'd been to Palermo, Spain, Switzerland, Germany, Holland, Belgium etc. He told about his wife who often hops over to France with him, and his two little girls aged three and five who sit on the engine in the cab. Great life. Wouldn't mind marrying someone like that.

The last lift was with an RAF man. His situation was awful. He had signed up twelve years' service carelessly, and now he has another nine to do yet, or else pay £200. The price of his freedom sold by his signature. What a life compared to that of the lorry driver above.

After I leave Jean in Bristol, I have more lessons in geography. My diary:

A Clarks' shoes lorry stopped for me. He told me that Street, in Somerset, is the largest shoe factory in England, and he said that last year they exported between seven and eight million pairs of boots and shoes to Russia. Now I don't know how many people there are in Russia, but I guess a high proportion of Russians must walk around in Clarks' shoes.

The next lift stops for me as I walked through Cullompton eating a huge Devon ice cream. A young man brings me all the way to

Torquay, where I sit in a café with Phil, who has met me after work in his hotel. Torquay is the kind of place that people from across England come to retire. My diary:

> Two older women were in the café. Both were pale and grey, with genteel London-sounding accents. One had egg and chips and the other had a double helping of apple pie. How she smiled when she saw that pie coming! They chatted about their houses and cleaning floors etc. While I ate my scrappy lunch, a lovely girl with enormous long flowing golden-ginger hair stopped and looked in the window. She wore slacks and a black sleeveless jacket over a purple sweater, and her hair swung in the Torquay breeze. I thought she looked great. The women started to talk, very loudly, about this girl. "What a lovely girl she is," said one. "And hasn't she got beautiful golden hair." "Oh," said the other weedy one, "I'm afraid I don't share your taste. Really if she's the young people of today – I don't share your taste at all." I pitied that woman in the dead-end-of-the-world town of Torquay and got up and left.
>
> When I tell Phil, he is more generous than me, and calls them "old dears".

Country Childhood
Hereford, 5 February 1966

In good moments, I find my life so exciting and wonderful that I confide in my diary:

> Everything feels so wonderful in bad or good ways that I get amazed that so much can happen to one person. Now last night, Mary and I sat chatting for hours about our childhoods in the country, the sadness and the beauties of everything we lived. The daffodils in my room started us off. We went back

to the snowdrops in the woods, how we worked on the farms and got to know and understand the ways of animals, how we watched our favourite calves grow into cows and have their own little ones, how we knew the hideouts of the foxes in the wood, the ferocious sparrow hawks and tiny wrens' nests in the woody banks. How we hated the people who came to kill the geese even though we feared the geese. The last remnants of an old way of life came back to us, things that our own children will not know because even now it's disappearing – the old woods are being dragged up and made into dull cornfields.

This morning, I'm lying on my bed looking around. For half an hour I looked at my pictures on the wall and in my books, and laughed and thought of everything, feeling intoxicated. Pictures of friends and people hitchhiking in Spain and Ireland and Africa and Northumberland and Wales. Every person there I love, every place swirls me away to the past. There are the Spanish dancing girls and the dusky sunset picture of camels in the Sahara, and how lucky we were to be there...

Gypsy violin music which is so beautiful it dances red and green before my eyes, and the lady daffodils in the room, and Phil in Devon now, and Jenny and Mary, and the boys in London and Ireland, and my family in Newcastle, and the hot golden desert in Africa. It's all the same to me.

And though I'm only an ant in the hugeness of everything, yet that ant's life couldn't have been much fuller. So full to bursting like elderflower wine that will soon shoot off the cork. Being a teacher is a good thought, because my kids can have what I've got if they want it.

One day I shall write a book. What about I don't know, but I know I'll do it because it's one way to burst out the cork.

Being Teachers
Hereford, 17 February 1966

It has to come – we are being trained to be teachers after all. Yesterday had been our big day. My diary:

> We all went off to the schools where we will be teaching all next half term, until Easter. Mine is at Bodenham, a country school a few miles from Hereford, and I only have seventeen children in my class. The teachers are all old, and so are the other two students that I'm with. Therefore I'm a bit spoiled. But it's nice to see people who are old-fashioned, who know they are and who don't mind being like that. The headmaster said I can do my Arab project. I can use as much music as I like, can do my psychology experiments and can in fact please myself. I'm very happy to be going there for five weeks.
>
> Mary is extremely pleased with her school and Tonie is bubbling over hers because it's Catholic and what she's used to.

Perhaps I'm not such a bad student as I thought I was. My diary:

> I'm very happy at the moment because I've been to see Mr Bennett about my psychology practical experiments, and he's happy about what I've done and says it should go OK. I'm investigating the "self concept" and have drawn a line of children from short to tall and another from thin to fat. In each case "normal" is in the centre. I will be asking children to place themselves along the lines. He said if I keep working hard, I should get a credit for Education. This is really unexpected, so I'm delighted. Though I do wonder how it came to pass, and it's not definite yet.

This notebook containing my diary is now filled up, and as I prepare to start the next one, I summarise our friends, focused on us in

Hereford, who are from Ireland, London, Cornwall, Birmingham and Newcastle:

This last half term has been a really excellent time. It has been the foundation of our now well-established gang which includes Ralph, Geoff, Len, Leo, Paddy, Gar, Steve, Brian, Dick, Rossie, Lorna, Philip, my sister Rosie, and here in Hereford Jenny, Janet, Mary and me and others, and of course my one and only charming little mouse.

We have five free days during half term, and we decide to gather in London.

THE CAPITAL
LONDON, 18 FEBRUARY 1966

I take my mouse in her wooden clog. My diary:

That mouse of mine is getting quite well travelled. She's been hitchhiking to Newcastle and back, and now will visit London and Berkshire. She sits in her little clog, tucked under my arm,

and stays there until we arrive, patiently tolerating the jolting of lorries and the awful noises, and sometimes coming out to sniff in intervals between lifts. I am hoping to get her a husband.

Mary went off to find a friend while I waited in Trafalgar Square for the others to arrive, which they didn't. Two policemen harangued me. "What is a nice young lady like you doing, hanging around here?" They wanted to know where I was from and who I was waiting for. I was getting colder and wetter. In the end I took a train to Geoff's.

I am feeling out of things at Geoff's. Len has arrived, and he and Jenny are having deep conversations. Rosie arrives from Newcastle, Philip from Cornwall and Pete from London. Although I am fond of them all, there is no special boy with whom I am perfectly at ease. Somehow Geoff's mother manages to accommodate all of us.

SUBURBAN HOUSE
CROWTHORNE, 18 FEBRUARY 1965

We all move, in various ways, to Jenny's home in Crowthorne, Berkshire, before returning inevitably to Hereford. It is quite different from the housing estate where Geoff lives. My diary:

It is big and roomy, with a garden all around in sort of quiet suburbia. It is like stepping back into Victoriana, except for Jenny's sister who is very "Mod", unlike us wild lot. Mouse is very at home here, and everyone is paying her a good deal of attention.

We are all installed in Jenny's house. A boy called Douglas has just come round, and from the point of view of Jenny's parents he is an ideal suitor. But he is hardly likely to appeal to her.

The old couple live surrounded by the treasures of their

past. They once had a tea plantation in India, and they are old colonial types, people who work hard for what they had and think of people in terms of what they worked for. Goodness knows how many ivory elephants, beautifully ornately carved wooden chests and tables, inlaid wooden boxes, plants and pieces from Brazil, India, France, everywhere. It's exactly like stepping back a hundred years to come into the house, and the shaggy tumbledown garden is full of secrets and patches. It's funny to think that they belong to the end of a type of English people whose ideas are out-of-date. Now these old colonials live their life of the past, in a once-rural part of the old country. And they retire and sink back into their dreams and forget that things are changing all around the thick, overgrown hedges of the house.

In the evening we crowded into a local pub and made our usual music. There were local men there, men of the soil who now lived in between the endless houses and estates, the last few who cycled and wore wellington boots, the last who had what they could call a "local". This part of England, all affected by London sprawl, is being suffocated by city growth.

Country School
Hereford, 1 March 1966

Mr Dance is the short, rotund, strict headmaster of the village school where I start my four weeks' teaching practice. Bodenham has four classes, and I am to take the oldest children of around ten years of age.

My class are country children, rosy-cheeked, willing, and well controlled by the watchful eye of Mr Dance. I am happy about the project I plan to do based on what I learned with Mary last summer in North Africa. And I hope to run a folk music club to practise the songs I've learned during my travels.

Mouse Courtship
Hereford, 4 March 1966

Mary has bought a white male mouse. We agree that it will fulfil my mouse's life if she becomes a mother. Mr Mouse is very enthusiastic. He rushes at his prospective mate excitedly as Jenny, Mary and I watch. She isn't going to stand for this behaviour, and defends her nest in the wooden clog, attacking him vigorously. The discomfited suitor is forced back. He circles around, pausing, looking, tiptoeing forward, retiring. It is a long while, an hour or two, before he learns better manners, slowly sniffing his way towards her. Finally, she agrees he may enter her clog, and we leave the pair alone.

Gypsy Family
Hay-on-Wye, 5 March 1966

After a week of teaching practice, we find the need to be on the move again. Mary goes to visit her family in Swindon while I hitchhike down to Hay-on-Wye to visit Betty, my friend from the gypsy Warner family who'd invited me to return. My diary:

The Warners live in a caravan in the corner of a field near Hay. They have been in Hay since at least 1876 when they are mentioned in Kilvert's diary. They are semi-settled gypsies though they still seem to get about a bit. Cecil's mother, old Mrs Warner, is absolutely ancient. I bet she doesn't know how old she is. She has the most wonderful brown wrinkled face, and pigtail ringlets around her ears. Both her daughters, Dorothy and Mary, are true-blooded gypsies, with fine dark skins and moulded faces. Cecil and Tommy, the sons, have twinkly eyes, outdoor skins, leathery bodies. The two men slipped off into the woods as the women talked, civilised maybe, but the light of artful lawlessness still sparkles in their faces and the creases of their grins.

Wales was very beautiful today. It was a warm sunny day, breezy too, and the mountains stood clear grey around every skyline. Birds were singing, white sheep were in green fields, yellow celandines in the thick hedges.

Betty and I were in the café having a cup of tea while doing some shopping. An Irishman rolled past the café door. When he heard me being called Bridget, and as usual associating my name with Brigitte Bardot, he said, "Vous parlez français, Brigitte?". I replied, "Oui, M'sieu, un peu." And he laughed heartily, thinking that very funny. He bought Ann Lewis, an irrepressible girl on probation, a cup of tea. She made lewd jokes and attacked everyone with good natured vehemence, keeping the whole place in hoots of laughter, while outside the birds sang, the cars roared past, and the usual village gossip seemed less catty than on an ordinary day.

Later, we were back at the caravan. Quietly, the evening cool was taking over the hills and fields all around, the little caravan at the centre of it all. Odd jobs were being done inside and out. The dogs were scratching around and Tony charging *through the field on his tiny tricycle. Somewhere out there, Cecil and Tommy were on business of their own between us and the river. I had to be getting back to Hereford. I waved goodbye to Betty, and little Tony ran along the field by the road, waving and telling me to come back again.*

That very same evening, at a college dance, Jenny and I decide that we don't fancy any of the men who have been invited to our all-girls establishment. They seem so weak and weedy. We prefer rougher, tougher lads, and ones who sing. My diary:

From sheer lack of other excitement, Jenny and I went round charging a sixpence parking fee from all the drivers as they left their cars in the car park. We felt guilty because everyone was taken in so easily, so we usually gave it back. But I've learned one thing. The kind of men I like don't go wriggling around in girls' college dances. I felt an instinctive dislike of the officially-approved method of meeting men last night.

The Black Lion
Hay-on-Wye, 12–13 March 1966

The boys just don't seem to be able to stay away. My diary:

> I am passing along a street in Hereford when I see Leo from Dublin walking along.
> "Yahoo, Leo," I yell.
> "Hiya, Bridge."
> "When did you come down?"
> "Oh, got here about 8.00. Didn't have you girls' telephone number."
> "Who else is coming?"
> "Ralph's on his way. Geoff and Gerry may turn up."

Ralph joins us from London. Jenny, Mary and I decide to go with them all to Hay. My diary:

> We spend most of the evening in the Black Lion and all the Warner family are there, including the old grandmother and the two daughters. We accommodate ourselves in the same barn as last time. The same farmer finds us in the morning, but we haven't done any harm and he leaves us be. We leave and wander round in the drizzle looking for an open shop through the empty early Sunday morning streets of the town. Funny how everyone loves Hay besides me. In Bryne's shop in Bear Street, we buy milk and lemonade and drink it outside the closed Black Lion. The boys buy their Sunday papers at the Half Moon inn. We make our way through the quiet town to the river, and along the path through the woods. We sit by the water watching the fishermen, Mary and I singing and playing hymns on our various instruments. Leo climbed a tree to a great height, and Ralph made a little boat to sail on the river.
> We went back to the town for breakfast in the Wye

Café. Jimmy Maughan told us the story of Mr Armstrong, a solicitor who murdered his wife with arsenic, and then he murdered another solicitor Mr Martin. Jimmy's uncle, Mr Cheese, stood for days up in Hay's clock tower observing what went on in the streets around until Mr Armstrong was convicted. All this took place forty years ago. Jimmy with undoubted pride said Mr Armstrong was one of the greatest murderers in the country.

After breakfast, we return to college; the boys must hitchhike to London, and we are left trying to prepare for tomorrow's teaching practice.

Oh Adventure!
Hereford, 19 March 1965

Even though we are in our schools teaching during the week, at the weekend I decide to drop my pen and books. My diary:

Off I went, singing from my heart towards Wales, beautiful Wales, and its mountains in the spring sunshine. Cross the border and I feel one step nearer to heaven. Over those rolling Beacons into the Welsh colliery valleys I go, past black slag heaps and rows of cottages. How green was my valley, but how human it is now. Through Ystradgynlais and on to Swansea, always with a song, down through Swansea and onto the Gower Peninsula. Round by the silver bays glinting with too many rich people's cars. Back up near Llanelli, the town that Bethan, my Welsh-speaking friend comes from, beside the steel works, Pontardulais, Fforest Fach, past high thin chimneys, tired now but still with a song and a laugh into the green of Carmarthenshire. Night now, heading homeward, and what a dreamy journey under the brilliant stars. Walk a bit, be carried a bit, and gradually a hundred miles becomes fifty, and fifty becomes twenty. In Hay now, I stopped at the Warners' trailer. Gave Betty the photographs, and she gave me some chocolate. Two candles alight in her caravan, and the sleeping boy on his bed. It was quiet and warm, and I became warm with welcome. But time was against me, so I left and had more starlight walks until I reached Hereford.

Poor Jenny was ill in the sickbay, but I crept in and told her all my adventures. Oh Adventure, I'm your willing slave. May life always be exciting.

Rural School
Hereford, 21 March 1966

I am discovering that perhaps I do have some vocation to be a teacher. I am running a lunchtime folk music club as I'd hoped to, and Sarah, a friend from college, brings her guitar to sing with the children.

One day, my assessor from college comes in to check how I am doing. My diary:

Miss Patton came into my first muddly maths lesson where everybody was doing something different. In English, we wrote out the invitations to the play which is now called The Caliph's Great Disappointment by unanimous decision.

After lunch, the whole class trooped out to view the Bodenham landscape from Dinmore Hill, and we had great fun reconstructing the sea-covered, desert-covered, ice-covered, flood-covered landscapes all around us. Even playing rounders afterwards was quite fun. It was a beautiful day and we all enjoyed it. Teaching is really worthwhile when your children are as great as these, and you can teach them interesting work.

BABIES
Hereford, 25 March 1966

I discover that my mouse has given birth. I take Mr Mouse from his wife and return him to Mary in case he decides to eat his babies. Three days later, when it is safe to look at her nest, I discover that she has had at least five young ones. She scratches around in her box, seeing to all her domestic affairs, and the little ones squeak now and again. I cover the open orange box on the windowsill of my blue bedroom with a cloth when I leave, and the cleaners have never looked underneath to discover Mouse's home.

PERFORMANCE
Hereford, 29 March 1966

The day has come when my class is to perform their play. It tells the story of a beggar boy, Ali, who escapes with Malika, the girl he loves, to the Caliph's disappointment and the children's delight. The girls dance to my record of Arabic music, and the boys play my tin whistles, the Moroccan drum and a tambourine. They have learned how to prepare mint tea in the playground for the feast, using Mary's and my *djellabas* and our Moroccan teapots as props. My diary:

> The infants and juniors trooped out into the playground expectantly. I demanded perfection, of course, but everyone enjoyed the play. The dancers were really the star performers. The children spoke up well enough, and a few technical hitches were well covered up. We were entertained to orange squash and biscuits afterwards which I think was the children's favourite part. They all said they wished they could do Drama next term, so at least in that aspect of teaching practice I have had some success.
>
> We finished off the day with an International Musical Festival, in which Scotland won first and second prize, and Northumberland came third.

It has all been greatly worthwhile, and I am encouraged to think I will enjoy being a teacher. I know that first I must travel much more, but along the way I'll collect songs and stories and learn about the landscape, all of which will enhance my career.

The Pain Of Love
Hereford, 31 March 1966

Phil has come to Hereford from his job in Torquay. The spring weather is pulling us out onto the road more than ever, but hard things must be decided. My diary:

> I'd been looking forward to seeing him. But soon, I became realistic and knew that I couldn't go out with him any more because we were too far apart in interests and life, and this is mainly because of the terrific age-gap that separates us. It was difficult indeed to say it, and it was a horrible electric

situation. But I've had so many of these situations now, for me or against me, that I sat through it. For him, it was the first big shock of his life.

I am sad as he leaves and I hear the music of Joan Baez in my mind. She sings, in French and English, about the joys of love, which are but a moment long while the pain endures a whole lifetime.

It feels that way. But we must shake ourselves and look ahead.

POETRY
HEREFORD, 1 APRIL 1966

On April Fool's Day, the last day of term, I write a poem.

Amid the turmoil of packing a few things
To take to a foreign land
I am dreaming
Of all that life has granted me.
Too much, too many joys,
How dare I be so lucky.
My journeys over land and sea
Ever present mystery.
Joys in the winding streets in Wales
Are among my favourite traveller's tales
And I have crossed full many a land
From Holland's waters to Sahara's sand.
I have laughed for many a day,
I may have a tear, it will go away.
For joys and sorrows are a traveller's daily bread
As a cushion or a stone may be her nightly bed.
Tomorrow I leave my comely home
To travel through England and cross the foam.
With one final thought – I cannot write a poem!

9

Holy Week

Spain, Easter 1966

Cheerio Bren. See you in Seville at eleven in the morning, at the cathedral, on Good Friday.

I write this in my diary in Hereford on 19 March 1966. Good Friday this year is on 8 April, three weeks away from the day when we wave Bren goodbye as she returns to Birmingham.

We take it for granted that we will find our way to Seville in the south of Spain. We may not have much money but we know the ways of the road. We are in the middle of our four weeks' teaching practice in Hereford schools, but once this is over we will be free as the air.

Spain continues to attract us: the exotic architecture, the hot-country fields of oranges and olives, the courtesy and the machismo of the Spanish boys, the warmth of the motherly women in the *pensiones*. We plan to visit Seville during the celebrations of Semana Santa, Holy Week. My sister Rosie and her friend Alicia and I have arranged to go together. Our plan is to meet Jenny and Bren, who have a different schedule, in Seville on Good Friday.

***

Mouse Family Boards Out
France, 2 April 1966

Jenny and I take my mouse and her babies to her mother in Reading, who has agreed to look after them while I go to Spain. I leave Jenny, who will follow later with Bren, and press on to meet Rosie and Alicia in Dover. We cross on the ferry and hitchhike across France, walking through the pleasant rolling plains and farmlands, looking at lovely cowslips and blue skies, see the excitement at Le Mans, which is hosting a car-racing event, and enjoy coffee in a tiny café along the way.

Lorry Drivers
Burgos, 3–4 April 1966

We freeze on Saturday night, get soaked in rainstorms during the day, and are so wet, stiff and aching by the time we get to the border post by 10 pm that we laugh at the sight of ourselves. My diary:

> *The frontier guards left us alone to sleep, or practically alone. They seemed to be very keen on turning up with offerings of cognac, bread and other food in the middle of the night. But at about 5 am they awakened us. They'd been looking out for lifts for us from the passing traffic, and had found a ride to Burgos, several hundred kilometres through Spain, with two Portuguese lorry drivers. With them, we passed up into the Cantabrian mountains which were green at this time of year. We drove for miles along a sort of plateau between ranges and stopped at a roadside fountain for a well-needed drink and wash. The Portuguese men were typical in their interest in amor, but they were friendly and kind, and not persistent. They took us to a Spanish transport café and here we had fresh bread and butter, coffee and biscuits.*
>
> *Our drivers, after several attempts at affection which*

we firmly resisted, amiably let us go in Burgos. This was the city where Chris, Mary and I had slept out in the streets last summer while waiting for a lift to Santander. Today we arrived in pleasant sunshine in the calm midday rush of people, neatly and gaily dressed. The soft fresh air was delightful, and the sunshine warmed us right through.

Spanish Ritual
Toledo and Bailén, 5 April 1966

From Burgos we are picked up by an English couple in a small camper van, and they take us almost as far as Madrid. My diary:

> We passed across the plains of rolling farmlands and little villages, and saw many black oxen pulling ploughs and harrows, and tough-looking peasants in navy denim clothes and black berets. The dry often desert-like plains and low hills were of various sandstones, limestones and chalky materials as far as we could see, and the views stretched often for twenty or thirty miles. Near Madrid, the scenery changed. We crossed the Sierra de Guadarrama, amazed by the fantastic granite mountains eroded in tors and boulders. This went on for miles, plains of boulders carved in the weirdest of shapes, useless for agriculture.
>
> In Madrid we were picked up by Michelle, an American girl who took us to Toledo. Together, we found a pensión for seven shillings and sixpence each per night which we knew was too much but we were too tired to argue, and too hard up to eat in the local restaurants.

In Toledo, we spend an hour or two admiring the architecture remaining from the days of the Moors. Since being with Mary in North Africa last summer, I relish seeing Arabic architecture here, considerably closer to northern Europe. But we can't linger. We are determinedly heading south, and still travelling with Michelle in her car. My diary:

> *The sun attempted to shine through low cloud as we crossed miles of plain away from the mountains of Toledo. There were spring flowers, green wheat fields, peasants with donkeys carrying loads of green grass. Unusual for me to see Spain being green.*
>
> *At last, we reached Nacional 4, the main road from Madrid to Andalusia. We whizzed south, and as it got dark we decided to stop for the night at Bailén, place of many unpleasant memories from our first visit in 1964. There we quickly found an inexpensive pensión.*

"Inglesas?" A man who is a local teacher befriends us in the *pensión*. He speaks English. When we tell him that we're heading for Seville and Holy Week, he says, "I'll take you to the procession in Bailén!" We are pleased to accept because we know we'll be less likely to be pestered if we are with a man. But first he can see that we need food. My diary:

> *He gave us wine and rare foods including salted, roasted almonds and peanuts, chips with odd sauce, and the others ate various fish including octopus.*
>
> *Eventually the music of a brass band could be heard, and numerous people thronging the streets began heading in a certain direction. To the solemn steady drumming of Boom Boom Ba, Boom Boom Ba-Boom, rows of women dressed in black were carrying candles. After them came the penitentes. Their three-foot high pointed black hats were like those of the Ku Klux Klan, with little eye slits and black shoulder length capes. Their bodies were covered*

with ankle length white robes so that only their feet could be seen. They moved along in rows, slowly swaying from side to side as they walked. The leading penitent held up a flag with the emblem of their brotherhood. After them came the figure of Christ mounted high on a wagon, with candles and glittering gold. The men carrying the wagon were hidden under coloured vestments. Sometimes the procession would stop and then someone in the crowd would sing a long wailing song to the Christ figure. When he'd finished, the procession moved on again, to the same repetitive rhythm of the drums. The figure of Christ was followed by more penitentes dressed in black this time, and they really did look frightening apparitions, those in front playing the drums.

Even though Rosie and Alicia are practising Catholics, and I too have been brought up with the church's rituals, this startles us. Why are these people being so penitent? Why this extreme reaction, presumably to the crucifixion story? What is it about Spanish culture that relishes such a tradition? We find it disturbing and even frightening. Although we expect to see more of this in Seville, tumbling into it in the small town of Bailén is a personal and unexpected experience. It seems to spring from the old pagan ceremonies.

At the end of this long day from Toledo to Bailén, Tuesday of Holy Week is over, and back at the *pensión* we fall asleep in a state of emotional exhaustion.

Oranges
Córdoba, 6 April 1966

There is no colour as orange as oranges. We wake early in the morning as noises draw us to our window. My diary:

Horse hooves are clattering on the cobbles below, Spanish voices carrying up to us, and hooting of lorries. In the market place directly below us is a huge open lorry piled high with the most beautiful round orange oranges imaginable. There are oranges piled all around the market place. Other vegetables too, but so many oranges.

We hadn't known there were so many oranges in the world. We'll have to find some and eat them.

Our friend of last night, who is a local teacher, appears and takes us to breakfast, where we have crisp freshly cooked *churros*, those fried sticks of dough that we'd first tasted in 1964. He buys us a hot drink tasting of aniseed. He assures me that I can come back to Bailén and teach English in the summer, if I'd like to.

Leaving him and the mountains of oranges behind, we set off towards Córdoba, the next stop on our way to Seville. This is springtime, and it must be the time of orange harvest. This is strange to us as our harvest is always in summer and autumn. The acres and acres of olive groves and orange orchards are filled with a riot of colour, the green overlaid with scarlet poppies, golden buttercups, marigolds, purple flowers, orange flowers. It is a wild, mad confusion. In Britain, where weedkillers are becoming a matter of routine for farmers, we would never see such an astonishing drama of colour.

Córdoba, that lovely town with the Alcázar, the Mezquita and the orange-tree-lined streets, no longer has a youth hostel. It has become a furniture shop. I leave Rosie and Alicia resting while I trail around in the heat but the *pensiones* are too expensive. Holy Week is putting up all the prices.

Rosie and Alicia are chatting with a tall fair-haired young man when I return to them.

"Bridget, this is Sergi," Rosie tells me. "He is from Catalonia." And as I collapse on our heaps of baggage he decides to take over our arrangements.

"Have you girls got a tent?" We shake our heads. "Perhaps you can hire a tent at the campsite," he suggests. But the man at the campsite shakes his head. Sorry, no tents for hire.

"Then, please, Sergi, ask if we can sleep on the campsite without a tent," I say. Although the man has never had such a request before, he agrees. We sleep easily under the moonlit sky, listening to the drumbeats of the processions. At home, under such circumstances, it would be sure to rain, but here in Spain it does not.

Next day, Alicia hitchhikes with Sergi and Rosie with me, and we arrive in Seville by midday. The journey has taken us four days from Dover and has cost us very little money.

I am asking myself the question, Why do we travel? Five days of constant movement, on the road, hitchhiking, walking, finding places to sleep, finding food to eat, all on the tiniest of budgets. And now we have arrived. Why do we do it? We are tired out, and I ask myself this. What is this sense of adventure I rave about?

Where will we sleep tonight? Seville is a huge city. There is no youth hostel, and we don't know the whereabouts of any campsites. We decide to look for the *pensión* that Mary, Chris and I stayed in during summer 1964. Nearly two years ago. Luckily, we find it.

"*Las señoritas inglesas!*" exclaims the woman whose expansive motherliness I recollect so well. She embraces me and then Rosie and Alicia. She remembers me and my friends, and understands that we are not rich tourists. She tells us that we can stay for forty *pesetas* a night. As the minimum price in Seville during Holy Week is eighty *pesetas*, we know how lucky we are.

PROCESSIONS
SEVILLE, 7–12 APRIL 1966

It is Maundy Thursday and, as practising Catholics, Rosie and Alicia go to the cathedral to make their confessions. Sergi and I are content to live with our sins, and we climb the Giralda tower, built when Seville was an Arabic city and the cathedral was a mosque. There are slopes upwards around the inner square edges of the tower instead of steps. We admire the shining white buildings and flat roofs of the old town.

The Semana Santa processions are drawing the crowds, and later all four of us mingle among them. We want to see it all. The crowds are so dense and tightly packed that people's bodies are pressing against each other. As the holy statues approach to constant drumming, the excitement level of the people rises, and we find out that the groping of women accompanies it. Is it just us, the foreigners, the fair-haired ones, who have to put up with it? We can't know. Slapping, pushing the hands away and loudly protesting, thinking to shame the gropers, none of this has an effect. Sergi is with us but it is hard to stay together.

So what are we to do? We always carry a few handy safety pins in our little bags for essential repairs. I open a pin and plunge the point into the body of the next groper. He responds with an outraged yell. A little later, the next offender gets the same treatment. They are as indignant as if we had offended them. Grope, plunge in the pin, yell – this is not the best way to experience the religious devotion of Spanish men. Aren't they ashamed to insult women in front of their beloved Virgin Mary and the other saints? It seems not.

The statues stop from time to time for someone to sing a plaintive song, as we'd seen in Bailén, but all is not totally melancholic. The men hidden under the great platforms bearing the statue of the Virgin make her dance by moving in a certain way, and everybody in the crowd thinks this is very funny. I am befuddled. I have always thought of religious devotion as something pious and respectful, not to be mixed up with grappling women and a dancing Mother of God.

Good Friday
Seville, 8 April 1966

Next day is Good Friday, and I head for the cathedral to meet Bren and Jenny as we had originally arranged. But, although I wait with Sergi for a couple of hours, they don't arrive. Meanwhile, Rosie and Alicia have been befriended by Juan and Manuel and are walking under the palm trees in the park together. Sergi now leaves for Madrid, and he and I exchange addresses. Perhaps I'll visit him in Catalonia on the way back to England. I feel sad and alone. Then an American backpacker called Tom approaches, asking if I can help him find accommodation for the night. We wander the streets together, but everywhere is full. Eventually, our kind lady at the *pensión* says he can put his sleeping bag on the floor.

Then it begins to pour with rain. The *pensión* roof is not watertight. Water drips steadily into buckets and bowls lining the corridors, and in our room too we need to dodge the drips. But who would complain? We are so lucky to have a roof over our heads.

Because of the non-stop rain, we learn that some of the Good Friday processions are cancelled. That is another odd thing about Catholic Spain. The Holy Week plans depend on hot dry weather. The statues are too valuable, presumably, to be damaged by rain.

Next day, the rain stops. How many processions do we really want to see? They seem to be going on all day, in different parts of the town. Tom and I wander around, sitting for hours under the scented orange trees near the cathedral, and soaking up the lovely heat.

"Bridget, why don't we travel through Spain together?" he asks at one point. "You could drop everything and just come."

This is totally impractical. I am with Rosie and Alicia, and I barely know him. But I feel it is hard being a girl. Spanish boys are at one extreme or the other, either courteous but distant, brutish or crude. English boys are dull. French boys are flirtatious and move too quickly. Tom has good conversation, easy-going manners and physical attractiveness. Of course I decline. When he leaves that evening for Madrid, I once again feel a gap. What am I doing here in Spain? Why am I travelling like this? What is the point of it all?

EASTER SUNDAY
SEVILLE, 10–11 APRIL 1966

Rosie and Alicia are off with their new boyfriends, Tom has left, and I am wandering around feeling uncertain. Jenny and Bren have not arrived although I check for them every morning at eleven o'clock. The Spanish males keep up the *"pss pss Rubia"* everywhere I go, and I'm getting fed up with this. But then I hear my name being called and who should it be but Manuel from Antequera, one of the boys Mary and I had made friends with last summer. This is just what I need to cheer me up. My diary:

He took me to an Easter Sunday dance where the Spanish young people were letting themselves go. Some were doing

Beatles-type dancing, tinged by their own flamenco style. Most did a smooch-cum-tango and I also was subjected to that. After the dance, and during it, we had a big discussion on Spanish and English morals, in which I was undoubtedly the winner. He shook hands, and I thanked him for the night which had been much better than I'd expected. Back at the pensión, I chatted with my kindly host and her friends. They gave me some bread, bananas and potato chips, and I was so hungry that I gobbled it all happily.

On Easter Monday, there is still no sign of Bren and Jenny outside the cathedral, so Rosie, Alicia and I decide to make a day trip to Jerez de la Frontera. We hitchhike off easily enough, and on arrival buy a glass each of the real sherry produced in the region.

"We'll do our shopping here," says Rosie when we find ourselves in the market place. "All good tourists buy souvenirs to take home!" We buy cow and goat bells, a horse's rope bridle, sombreros, a palm-leaf broom and huge donkey baskets to keep everything in.

We have reached as far south in Spain as is possible, and it is time to think about how we will get home.

I'll Go Alone
Córdoba, 12 April 1966

We have all our souvenirs from Jerez de la Frontera packed in the donkey baskets, our brooms, and our rucksacks with sleeping blankets tied on top. Three of us won't easily find lifts with all this gear if we travel together.

"I'll go by myself," I suggest. I fancy this. Being alone means I can walk along the roads at my own pace, stop when I want to, and keep my thoughts to myself.

"*Adiós, mi hermana, mi amiga,*" I say. Goodbye, my sister, my friend. "Perhaps we'll meet in Córdoba tonight. But if not, see you in *Inglaterra.*" We wave, and off I go. My diary:

> *Adventure I love, and I got it. When we parted I had about five shillings in Spanish money, about two shillings in French money, my boat fare across the Channel, five shillings in English money to see me through in England, and 2000 miles to do. That's a good challenge for me. I set off in top spirits, wondering how long I'd keep them up. Rosie and Alicia had quite a lot of money and were hitching together so I didn't worry about them even though it's their first day hitching alone in a foreign land.*

Five shillings converted into Spanish *pesetas* is enough to pay for a bed in a cheap *pensión* for one night, and leaves nothing for food or bus fares. I plan to visit Sergi in Sabadell along the way and have nothing but optimism to support my finances.

I soon arrive in Córdoba and the driver of my car delivers me to the reception of a student *residencia,* an inexpensive hostel. I can have a bed for thirty *pesetas* the night. That's good. I'll have a few *pesetas* left over to spend on food, I think. It has begun to pour with rain again. Santiago, who is a veterinary student, offers to take me out. I leave my bags by the front desk and off we go. We listen to modern jazz in a local club and do some smoochy-type dancing. This leads to discussion in mixed French and Spanish between northern and southern temperaments. I can see where this is leading. Santiago tells me I am *muy simpática*, very pleasing, and that he likes my green eyes even though they are blue. But what I really want to see, and have never had the chance, is some authentic flamenco. He knows what to do.

The Flamenco Restaurante is in the Judería Cordobesa, the Jewish Quarter. My diary:

> *We wandered off through the lit tiny streets to this place and ordered some vino dulce. There were five Spanish people performing, a man guitarist, a man singer, a young male dancer and two girls. It was truly fascinating. They twirled and shook and stamped and clapped their hands to the music. I was enthralled. The dancers were enjoying themselves so much. Santiago was always calling out Bravo, Olé.*

Never before, and never since, have I been anywhere where the flamenco was so perfect, so natural, so much performed for its own sake. At about one o'clock in the morning, it comes to an end, and Santiago takes me back to the *residencia*.

A matronly little woman greets us at the door. She is some kind of housekeeper and is obviously concerned for my welfare. I bid goodnight to Santiago, whose gentlemanly manners could not be faulted, and discover that I am sharing the little woman's double bed. I sleep soundly, and in the morning my friend brings me breakfast in bed. "*Nada, nada,*" she says. Nothing to pay. She has understood how little money I have, and my accommodation has cost her nothing. No extra sheets to wash. What could be more natural? I am humbled.

Land Of The Moon-Faced People
Albacete, 13 April 1966

I am travelling towards Valencia, on the Mediterranean coast through the province of Albacete. At first, I am enraptured by the countryside. My diary:

> *I travel through acres of olives, and under the trees are fields full of yellow flowers, then purple flowers, then scarlet ones, and the roadsides a mass of scarlet, gold and pink. Overhead are rolling clouds of thunder or patches of golden and blue sky, always changing as I move along, dreamily tired. Past Andújar, past Bailén, into new territory, unexplored I feel by hitchhikers, and I get the feeling of excitement that makes me wonder what is to be discovered in this central, isolated part of Spain.*
>
> *Before long I pass Linares and there are slag heaps from coal and iron workings dumped on a high, dry plateau of limestone. Industry, here, in this part of Spain – I hadn't expected it. On I pass, through many a green shady valley, over a huge expansive view across the mountains and plains of olives, and by every roadside the spare, precious grass is being piled into donkey baskets by peasant farmers.*

The two men in whose car I am riding are talking continually, and telling me unfavourable things about Albacete. I am so tired that it is difficult to speak and understand Spanish. My diary:

> *They laugh uproariously at my palm leaf broom. What on earth could I possibly want it for? My mother would turn me out! They laugh at a little village perched precariously on a bumpy mountain top, and they keep saying, "Don't go to Albacete, muy feo, muy feo. The women are fea and wear long dresses and have horrible faces. It is really very ugly. Why do you want to go there? Murcia, si. Alicante, si. Barcelona, si. But Albacete, nada, nada." As we approach the province of Albacete, they grimace even more horribly and laugh at the bumpy, wartlike surface of grey broken limestone mixed incongruously with red-brown soil and greenish weeds.*
>
> *The land gets even flatter as we move on and becomes so totally uninteresting that it's almost amazing. Albacete city can be seen from miles away, but when we get there, there are only straight flat squashed rows of houses, ugly policemen and ugly señoras. I am both exhausted and fascinated. I leave my Spanish driver friends in the darkness of the evening and approach a house which is advertising rooms. The one-legged moon-faced man talks to me but I can't understand what he is saying. Then a woman with the hugest imaginable rear end bends over in front of me, and about five moon-faced young bloods are in the room, being pleasant and addressing me as señorita. My heart thumps at the thought of those virile young fellows fathering dozens more like them.*
>
> *My excursion has brought me to the Land of the Moon-faced People. Perhaps I'll wake in the morning and find it all a dream*

Real Spain
Sabadell, 14 April 1966

It isn't a dream but it has a strange feeling. My diary:

> *The moon world was drugged and sluggish this morning. I felt that I'd been a moth in the darkness flitting in and out, while the moon people are plodding on regardless. I left at 6 am and headed for the high road again with the grand sum of 5 pesetas 80 centavos to my name, and 500 kilometres to Sabadell where Sergi lives, near Barcelona.*

I am now back in the real Spain again, of pestering men and orange trees. My diary:

> *Men mauling and leering, whining and pleading. I don't like pudding-faced men making eyes at me as in Moon Land; no more do I like podgy middle-aged dark Spaniards mauling. And I had both today. What a relief it was to get a long lift with a polite French boy with whom I could relax, and who said "Pardon" when he accidentally brushed my knee as he changed gear.*

The change from bare Moon Land to the plush lands around Valencia was as welcome to me as to a desert traveller reaching an oasis. Back in the rich green lands of cultivation where there are paddy fields of rice, acres of orange trees scenting superbly and often laden with beautiful waxen oranges. There were golden lemons too, and irrigated fields of tomatoes. Palm trees waved in the sunny breeze, and the peasants were lithe and brown at their work in the fields.

By very good chance I was dropped near an orange grove, and as I was really hungry I nipped inside and plucked a handful of oranges. That first bite was so delicious, golden sweet drops of sunshine trickling down my parched throat, fresh orange from the tree. I had some stale bread, and together with six oranges this made quite a meal.

I went miles with this French boy. At one point we ran out of petrol, so I hitchhiked back to a garage and came back with a container-full for him, having to cope with maulers along the way. But it was worth it. He took me almost to Barcelona, and from there I hitched to Sabadell to Sergi's family house where I had been invited to spend the night.

"Welcome, Bridget," says Sergi's mother. "He has told us about you. But why are you alone? Where are your sister and her friend?" I explain that we decided that being separate would make travelling easier. I have begun to sense that the Catalan people are culturally different. My diary:

They are not Moon Men and not Latin or Arab-type people. They are tall, polite and intelligent. The man who brought me all the way to Sergi's house was kind, and so was Sergi's family. They gave me a well-needed meal. It was good to see him again, with that comforting feeling of having friends in Spain.

> *In the evening, I went with Sergi and his younger brother to their friends' house and was told that they'd take me and show me another side of Spain the next day.*

Next morning, Sergi, his younger brother Javier and his friend Ramon take me to a slum satellite settlement called Torrent del Capellà. They are socialists, they explain. It is made clear to me that, although this is not illegal, Spain is not a free country, and one must be careful. They talk darkly about the political party La Phalange. I feel like a foreign MP or important person being shown around. They point out the poverty, the barefooted children in ragged clothes who should have been in school and the lack of sanitation. The sun is shining, and in this warm dry climate, I mention that we have slums in Britain too, where the cold and damp create a different kind of misery. Nevertheless, Sergi and his friends point out that improvements are necessary, and they are keen for me to understand that changes must take place in Spain.

Tiny Country
Andorra, 15 April 1966

By midday, I am ready to depart. I have chosen the most difficult of all the routes to cross the Pyrenees, because although I have almost no money I want to visit Andorra. This tiny principality seems to be in neither France nor Spain but on the border between the two. I head north along what looks like the main route through Manresa and Gironella. My diary:

> *The lack of cars was amazing. The Pyrenees grew more beautiful as I mounted higher and higher, and there was a good deal of snow on the mountain tops. I crossed the border into France, and was very happy, singing all the time. The mountains then grew so fantastically high and steep sided that the roads curved tremendously and were very dangerous.*

Although Andorra is a tiny country among the highest part of the Pyrenees, it must have miles of roads to get short distances.

I crossed the border back from France into Andorra with two Catalan men smugglers. They bought lots of stuff out of a frontier shop, piled in bags and boxes under a blanket. They were not stopped by the border guards, and it seemed that my presence in the car was a help.

It is getting towards evening when they drop me off at the main town, Andorra la Vella. I enquire but discover that even though this is a tourist destination there is no youth hostel. The place is full of hotels, but they are beyond my means.

"Now, Bridget," I lecture myself, "you've romanticised many times about the glamour of the road, of busking, so get out your tin whistle and see if you can earn some money."

I feel awkward, but I do. The odd-looking fair-haired English girl that I am, I sit cross-legged on the pavement in the town centre, lay my red beret on the ground, and begin to pipe a few Irish jigs. I never have got them off to perfection, but I hope no-one will realise. Most of the passers-by ignore me, although some give me looks of surprise. No-one puts any money in my beret, and as my fingers begin to get colder and colder I realise this is not going to work. I haven't enough talent. This is not the right place, nor the right weather, nor the best time of day. So where am I going to spend the night?

I decide to ask at a hotel if I can work for a place to sleep for the night in my sleeping blanket. At the first one I try, the young man at the reception desk decides to help me.

"Wash dishes? We don't need anyone. But I'll take you to my friend who'll help you." We walk to a nearby hotel, where his friend puts me in a clean room with a stream rushing by outside the window. The two young men then treat me to a huge meal of Spanish *tortilla de patatas* with bread, butter and wine. A new resolution begins to form in my mind. My diary:

I am very thankful but I feel guilty. In future I resolve to have enough money not rely on people's kindness to me because I'm a young helpless female.

This resolution is for the future. For now, I must manage to get home with what I have. My diary:

I am up and out from my hotel room by 7.30, and spend my five and a half Spanish pesetas on a loaf of bread and a small bar of chocolate. I feel like a queen, spending that much money. The funny thing was that I've had this money, worth about eightpence, for two days now, and I've always saved it whenever I felt hungry for worse times to come, like a starving beggar who always has a coin in his pocket. What an odd thing it is to be really short of cash!

On I walked right through Andorra la Vella town, with one shilling and ninepence in francs to get me through France.

"Two-Horse" Car
Paris, 16 April 1966

What happens next seems a kind of miracle. I stand for ten minutes on the edge of town in the early morning sunshine, looking at the beautiful surrounding mountains, when along comes a car. It is one of those little Citroën *deux chevaux* cars that so many young people drive in France. They are rattly little things, with canvas seats suspended on metal frames.

"*Vous allez où, M'sieu?*" I ask, noting the French numberplate. Where are you going, sir? The driver looks at me quizzically. "*Je vais à Paris!*" he says. I'm going to Paris. This is unbelievably good luck. He rearranges his luggage and stows it with mine in the back. And I settle down for the 700-kilometre ride. My diary:

Paris! In one lift! I could hardly believe my luck, though things like this always seem to happen to me when I need them.

It had snowed in the night and climbing the upper reaches of the mountains in that little car was quite tricky. But it was beautiful. Skiers were coming out in droves, although it was too early to see anyone actually skiing.

My companion was a young French boy and he was really very quiet. Considering I was in his car for fifteen hours, I'm sure we never passed more than about ten sentences. I decided not to bother him with my scintillating conversation, and it was good to be peaceful anyway.

We descended from the high mountains to the foothills of the French Pyrenees and away from the snow. Before long, we were on an entirely flat land and zooming off northwards through the wide river plains of France. Being in France seems almost like home. It is the tenth time I've been through some part of the country now, if not entirely across it.

We passed Montauban and on to the edge of the Massif Central, and there was the River Dordogne. We passed Limoges, Bourges, Orléans, and by 11.15 pm we reached the southern outskirts of Paris. I was too tired to think of hitchhiking into Paris – I'd planned to stay with a friend called Bill – and anyway he may not have been in, it being Saturday. So when the French boy (we hadn't got to the point of exchanging names yet) said I could stay at his house, I thankfully accepted. His mother was very kind, and we had a most delicious meal of macaroni cheese with bread and butter, ideal for me. Now I'm going to sleep in a comfortable bed in the same room as a squeaking bird.

Over The Channel
London, 16 April 1966

I still have my few *francs* unspent. My diary:

> *I was sad that I couldn't stay in Paris, but zipping full of high spirits, and having the money for my métro fare, I ride to Porte de la Chapelle station to continue my journey home.*
>
> *A car with a GB registration pulls up. As we are on the road north, direction England, I say, "Are you going to Calais?"*
>
> *"Yeah," smiles a man from under his hat.*
>
> *"Have you got room for me?"*
>
> *"Yeah, sure, we can squash you in."*
>
> *"Yippee," said I, and before long I was on my way to Calais.*
>
> *We caught the ferryboat with minutes to spare, and suddenly we were in Dover. The men took me to their friends' house where we had sandwiches and strong tea with milk. What more could anyone want?*
>
> *By 11 pm we were in London where I left my new friends. I am not sure where I can stay the night. Uncertainly, I telephone my grandmother. Surely it is a bit too much to land on my seventy-year-old grandmother, unexpectedly, at this time of night. But she is amazingly good and tells me to come to her house. I have enough money for the underground and bus fare, but I realise I am up to my old beggar tricks again. I'll have to think hard about this.*
>
> *It is wonderful to be at Gran's. It is good to be home in England and talking to people I love in a language I know. Anyone would think I'd been away years, not just two weeks.*

Mouse Family
Crowthorne, Monday 18 April 1966

I must go to Jenny's house first to see why she didn't meet us at Seville, and also to check on my mice.

My diary:

How the mice have grown. There were seven youngsters, all fat and healthy. I had to sell them though as I haven't anywhere to keep them for the next two weeks. Camberley pet shop took them, but I kept my beautiful grey mother mouse and one of her white babies. Jenny explained that she was on her way to meet me in Spain, even though she never arrived.

I make a map in my diary, and summarise it:

Hitchhikes to date – 2 April to 18 April
 Hereford through France, to the south of Spain, Andorra, France again and England.
 3061 miles or 4,900 kilometres in 16 days.

10

Towards The Peak

WALES, IRELAND, HEREFORD, SUMMER 1966

WALES, WALES
GLASCWM, 7 MAY 1966

The most beautiful part of the world to me is the Welsh borderland. I wake up in my blue room on a lovely May morning, eat a good breakfast, wish Mary and Jenny best of luck as they struggle with their essays, feed the mice, and set out. My diary:

> *I hitched out along the familiar A438 as far as Clyro, had a great couple of lorry drivers, and got into the swing of being a hitchhiker again for a bit. However, I felt like walking today, in the mountains.*
>
> *From Clyro village I climbed, puffing and panting, really out of condition, until eventually I got used to it again and began striding out. There were lovely views south from Clyro Hill, down to the Wye valley, Hay, and up into the Black Mountains, and I could see Mynydd Troed and Pen-y-fan right into Wales. Once over Clyro Hill, I met a different scene,*

the green quilted wild and rounded hills of Radnorshire. There was Bailey Bedw, Top o' Lane and Painscastle, the countryside of my childhood. Then I went down to Rhosgoch and up to Hondon where my father used to take the bees to the heather in those long gone days. Up into the hills, really into new country now, I tracked miles of heather, bracken and whinberries in really desolate hills, then down into the green narrow valley of Glascwm.

There were white shining farmhouses, a tidy little church, a triangular shaped green, and a post office. The youth hostel is the old school, tiny and utterly charming. It's a long time since I was in a hostel, almost a year since I was in a British one, and the familiar bits and pieces were very pleasant to see and smell again.

I found a book, the Trapp Family Singers. I cooked two eggs, a bit of cheese, ate them with two apples and an orange, went for another a walk for a couple of miles, heard a cuckoo on the hill, also a grouse saying Go-back, Go-back, Go-back. There are lots of sheep with darling lambs everywhere. This place is really the place to come to get away from twentieth century pressures.

I woke to the call of the cuckoo and the bleat of lambs, accompanied by the steady drip of the rain. My breakfast was meagre, so I was really hungry and lacking in energy to climb those hills. However, I forced myself up endless miles of round broad-backed mountains. It was so beautiful and isolated, with the curlew calling and irate seagulls swooping over the mountain tops. By the time I reached the valley that separates these hills from Radnor Forest, I was very hungry, so hitched back to Hereford. Radnorshire is the most beautiful part of the world to me and I'd like to go back there eventually.

Ireland Beckons Again
Boyle, 26 May–4 June 1966

It is the Whit week holiday and time for the next *Fleadh* in Ireland. I have fitted in some work on my various college projects, but I must escape again. My diary:

> *I fitted up my rucksack with my pipes, a saucepan, a mug, compass, bottle opener, made piles of sandwiches, contrived pounds of biscuits, cake, fruit etc to last me. So what with stores I'm carrying and coffee I'm going to make, and ten shillings I'm taking for at least a week, I may just about manage.*
>
> *It's a lovely evening now. The sun is setting over Wales, the birds are singing outside, the mice are happy on the windowsill, I'm all cheerful with my scarlet dress on, dreaming ahead of all the adventures of the next six days.*

Early in the morning, I am on the road north from Hereford, and just outside Leominster a lorry picks me up going all the way to Liverpool. Becky and Jan have left before me, and my lorry picks them up too. He deposits all three of us at Liverpool docks by 1.30 pm. My diary:

> *We had time until the 10.15 pm ferryboat to fill in, so we decided to explore the docks. This meant getting an official permit, and judging by the looks we got from the dockmen, girls can't be given permits very often. We saw the amazing variety of goods which come in and out of Liverpool, and we went round an Irish cattle boat, and watched a Swedish tanker being filled with lard.*

As we line up in long queues for the tickets, Ralph arrives from London. The boat is so crammed that even getting a sitting place on the floor is difficult, and we have a nine-hour journey ahead of us. Surely everyone can't be going to the *Fleadh* in Boyle, where we are heading? My diary:

> Before long I was talking to a pleasant Irish chap from Dublin, and then we heard the musicians strike up Irish ceilidh music, and all the Irish people began to sing and dance. There were fiddles, pipes, spoons, an accordion, and this went on half the night. As we were tired, we all squashed together on the deck to keep warm. Sleep was not really possible. The journey seemed long as daylight approached, but eventually we sailed into the Liffy estuary and between the rows of docks into Dublin. In the squash of getting off, I lost my Irish lad which was a bit sad. However once in Dublin, we were filled with energy and raring to go.
>
> Becky hitched with Ralph and I with Jan. We left Dublin walking along the Liffy side and through O'Connell Street. All the people were hitching to the Fleadh, creating a terrific atmosphere. Jan and I passed Becky and Ralph in a lift, and our driver picked them up. We soon were well on our way to Boyle. At one point, Jan and I went separately, while I was going along by the Shannon passing the lovely stretches of water.
>
> The Fleadh was just like last year, people arriving from all over Ireland with rucksacks, musical instruments, bottles. The weather was really sunny and we sat around looking at the crowds. Then the ceilidh music started up, the tinkers began to set up their card tricks and there was dancing and general gaiety. At one point Jan and I were feeling a bit lonely. Suddenly June and Annette and all our girl friends from Dublin turned up. We made a camp with them and cooked some supper. Then Len turned up with Damien, and we all felt happy. We had drinks. We sang. The music was really good, and the streets were packed.

This is the first time I've seen Damien since the *Fleadh* in Thurles in June 1965. He had never joined the visits to Hereford College with the other boys, and I am pleased to see him with Len. He has a twinkle in his eye, a way of smiling sideways as he tells his stories. Both boys are wearing their Aran sweaters as I had expected. My diary:

> Next day was the same, swimming in the river to cool down, drinking outside the pub, listening to the music and soaking in the sunshine.
>
> Suddenly we heard the sound of the highland bagpipes echoing through the air. Along came the bands, some Scottish, some Irish, children playing whistles and accordions, women's bands, girls' bands, then lorries with Irish-costumed people on them and fiddlers. Everywhere there were yells of delight from the spectators. And so it went on for the rest of the Fleadh. Continuous festivities of music, drinking, good crack and goodwill everywhere. The spirit of jubilation and friendship is wonderful. The weather held out as it has never

done before. We were all so happy, especially us from cool, repressed England.

In the middle of Monday night, after a simply wonderful time with music and fiddlers and warm moonlit air, the boys had to leave for Dublin for work the next day.

We girls followed at a more civilised hour on Tuesday morning, which happened to be market day. Calves were being shepherded around the streets, and cows, piglets, and little donkeys pulling carts. Still in hot sunshine, we left Boyle and hitched to Dublin. Jan and I had a long lift in a chip van, and we got filthy and simply covered in grease. In Dublin, we met Len, Damien and Gar, and then Gene with his friend who brought us some sandwiches.

It was a sad group of English people who sailed down the Liffy into the broad sea, waving goodbye to Dublin and the hills of Ireland below a golden crowning sunset. The seagulls screeched, the sea was calm and striped with red reflections as we left Ireland for probably a long while.

Serious Work
Hereford, 5 June 1966

My diary:

> Plans for the big adventure of the future are everywhere in the air. Poland, Austria, who knows – that is me. My sister Helen in Newcastle is soon getting married. She is two years younger than me and has succeeded in finding a man in a way that I have not. Jenny and Mary have had interviews for teaching in Birmingham. My little blue-painted room in the corner soon won't be mine any more, and my mouse on the windowsill, with her babies, will have to be cared for by someone else. All my things except for a few personal possessions will be sold off, and I will possess nothing except the proceeds of the sale. My record collection will be packed away silent and unloved for a year, which is how long I anticipate that I'll be gone. Soon, my friends and I will have a final Fleadh at Hay-on-Wye and then we'll all be going so many ways. The challenges facing all of us in the future are so exciting, and we don't know but we think our friendships will survive it all.
>
> All weekend, Jenny and I have been very lazy. We've read interesting books, had stimulating conversations with ourselves and other people, listened to music, eaten nice food, danced wildly to different types of music. I had a very absorbing Sunday morning trying to master difficult Irish jigs on my whistles which annoys other people. Then Jenny and I listened to ancient Chinese music tonight. If I had more time, I should like to study the development of music from primitive onwards and go round the world with a tape recorder. I began learning some Polish, struggling with Cz and Sz, and other difficult sounds, and revised a little about Dewey and his decimal system.

Special Study
Hereford, 8 June 1966

Despite various trips escaping from college, I have completed my special study of the two parishes in Britanny and Cornwall, made coloured maps on big sheets of card, written up my field work and handed it in. Our beloved geography lecturer, Mr Thompson, has left for another post, and this means that we present our work to Mr Tidswell. My diary:

> My big news of the day is that I got B+/A− for my special study. It was hardly comprehensible to me. I was perfectly dumbfounded. At most I'd expected B−. Mary got C+, and we were all pleased about that "plus". It means that we're sure now that Mr Tidswell wasn't being vindictive.

We had both done a vast amount of work to achieve this, two trips to Britanny and two more to Cornwall, to their mayors' or council offices and local libraries. Some of the research had been done in French, and even a little in Breton. We'd hitchhiked to our destinations, slept in barns and tramped over fields and hills. Our result has justified Mr Thompson's tentative faith in us. What a lot of work it has been. The course assessor looks it all over, summarising it in a few brief sentences:

> Miss B Ashton
>   This was an enterprising and interesting subject. The general presentation is very good, and many pieces of mapping are both excellent cartography and good geography. The use of photographs is sound.
>   The writing is clear but would profit in parts from greater length and thought.
>   S. M. M.

I wonder how much time and attention S. M. M. had spent on the assessment. Not a lot, I think.

EDUCATION EXAM
HEREFORD, 9 JUNE 1966

We must pass our education exam if we wish to qualify. My diary:

> *The exam doesn't frighten me. Mary is a bag of nerves, Jenny calm and flustering alternately, and the general air everywhere around is of excitement and hysteria. Other college work has been so pressing that no-one has really had time to do any swotting. We're all in the same boat. The "education" involved – branches of sociology, psychology, social psychology and philosophy – is all so full of complex concepts and complicated material that our lack of knowledge is the only thing that's obvious to anyone.*

DONE
HEREFORD, 10 JUNE 1966

It is over. My diary:

> *You can't even guess how well or badly you've done. All I know is that material which has flooded in during the past week came pouring out on paper in a sort of liberating bursting-free process, in no apparent kind of organisation. For me it was a release and a challenge too, to cope with those very deep and complex questions in the time allowed... I should pass, and so should most people I suppose.*

Deadlines
Hereford, 11 June 1966

Today I am working non-stop on my psychology experiment. It must be completed by next Friday for Mr Bennett, but I'd do anything for him, my ideal man.

I send off my final visa application for Poland. And I listen carefully to what Henry, Sarah's Polish boyfriend, is telling me about photography, and how I might find it worthwhile getting a good camera so that I can reproduce articles to be published in magazines when I get back from my travels.

Over the next few days, there is the tension between last-minute lectures, work to be handed in, and the pending freedom that awaits us. Mr Tidswell, our geography lecturer, is fighting a losing battle trying to interest us in Dutch ports. I have my first letter from Poland, sent by the Polish Youth Hostel Association, in an envelope with big foreign stamps. It includes information about crossing Soviet East Germany, which sounds both frightening and exciting.

Dreaming
Hereford, 15 June 1966

In our student hostel, overlooking the great lawn in front of the big red college building, I ponder my place in the world. My diary:

> *The night is still and warm outside, heavy and scented with flower smells, thick and exotic as in a Mediterranean town. Even though it's midnight, it's not dark, and a moon must be rising soon. England seems to carry the breath of foreign places. Before I came in, I was lying on the flat roof. Jenny and Mary were making tea inside. I heard them chattering and crockery clattering. Out there, I was wrapped in a blanket on the hard roof, dreaming as I might dream if I were under a foreign sky, sorting out star patterns between the clouds, knowing my*

direction to anywhere. An aeroplane passed. I worked it out as perhaps coming from Belfast and going towards Paris. All those people up there in that speck of light, moving through the air. I could see the interior of the plane, drowsing bodies, cigarette smoke, chatting, and people with books. How near, how far away, how close I felt to them. "'Night Bridge", said Jenny as she went downstairs. "Night Jen", I said. Everything seemed very worthwhile. I picked up the blanket, said goodnight to Mary, gave my mice some milk, and went to bed.

DISTRACTIONS
HEREFORD, 18 JUNE 1966

There are essays and pieces of work to finish and hand in, but inevitably there are distractions. We girls in Hereford are attracting the London boys yet again. My diary:

Jenny came rushing down the corridor as I was slumbering peacefully about 9.30 am. "Bridge – guess who's just woken me up? Ralph and Leo throwing stones at the window." A whole crowd of them came from London. With Ralph and Leo were Geoff, Gerry and another boy Joey. Gar turned up later, independently. It was a hotch-potch sort of a day. Becky and Jean went out with the boys, but I was too tired, and Jenny and Mary were working. Later, I went shopping for my big adventure and bought material for two dresses. In the evening, while they all went out, I sat snippety snip with my sewing things, and designed, cut out and pinned, fitted, sewed up and completed my red dress before going to bed. It's quite nice too, bright plain scarlet and straight fitting.

These boys are still being drawn in towards us in Hereford, this life that will last for only a few more weeks.

In Trouble
Hereford, 20–21 June 1966

Some workmen have been digging trenches for pipes between our hostel and the dining room. We must pass them on our way to eat, and we exchange banter. Interaction with working men? This must be the last straw for our superiors, who are trying to bring us up to be young ladies. My diary:

> As I drowsed peacefully on my bed in the early afternoon, I was awoken with a terrible shock. "Miss Hipwell would like to see you in her room, immediately!" "What, Margaret?" "Yes, and Mary and Tonie too," said Margaret. What have we done, we thought as we spruced ourselves up and sat waiting in the secretary's room. We were taken to the principal's office, one by one, and accused a) of causing trouble in the geography department, b) childish behaviour in and around the hostel – "I thought you'd have grown up by now but it seems you haven't!", and c) behaving generally irresponsibly. "Don't you realise that no headmaster will want to employ teachers whose standards are so low." Miss Hipwell says if I don't become less childish she will be compelled to inform my employing authority who will not want an irresponsible teacher on their books. Then she sends us off to apologise to the lecturers concerned.
>
> We were cool and resentful at the treatment we received and saw no reason to accept Miss Hipwell's standards. We think that outward appearances are not so important as inner qualities, and we see no harm in running and jumping around, singing, or talking to workmen which seems to be one of the greatest crimes.
>
> Miss Moore, with her red fingernails and black hair piled up in a bun, started to talk about standards, but when we asked her why we were being forced to accept standards we did not accept as right, she said that she had learned

> to conform too, and accepted it as part of her professional status. She outlined why people like us were nothing but a nuisance in the community, a community which we had joined from our own choice. I decide that I will try to be a bit less un-cooperative in future.

Later the same day, I confide in my diary:

> At twenty-one years of age, life spreads out in front of me, and I have never been so exhilarated at the sheer thought of living. In less than three weeks I'm beginning my journey around the world, something I've looked forward to for years. I take it quite for granted that I'm going. I'm busy preparing everything, and when the implications of what I'm doing suddenly hit me, my blood surges hot all around me, and a big fearsome joy and love of adventure fills me.

The very next day, more excitement. My diary:

> Oh joy of my life. There was a registered letter for me from the Polish Consulate, enclosing my passport stamped with a Polish visa. I rushed off to tell everyone. After tea I made a passport bag to carry my valuables around my waist and a grey denim shoulder bag to carry oddments in.

Results
Hereford, 22 June 1966

Now comes the time for our overall final geography assessment. All our essays, our special studies, our general attitudes to work and lectures, will contribute. Now is the time to display our Spanish land-use survey, made in summer 1964, when Mary, Chris and I noted the crops we passed by, using the milestones from south to north. We make a six-foot-long chart, and stick on hundreds of little rectangles showing the crops, or rocky territory where that applied. It is without doubt a work of art. Exactly what credit we will get for this masterpiece I am not sure. It certainly shows our interest in landscape and farming in Spain. Mary's and my maps from our special studies showing the maps and mountains of North Wales and the Massif Central, of Cornwall and Britanny, are on display.

I find out that I have managed a B+ for my psychology experiments. The result shows that the children's self-concepts tended towards the mean, rather than the extreme. The fat ones thought they were less fat, and the thin ones less thin. The tall ones thought they were less tall, and the short ones less short. Mr Bennett's only criticism was that there needed to be a greater number of children to give validity. One way or another, despite Miss Hipwell's criticisms, we all seem to be getting through the course.

My Sister's Wedding
Newcastle, 29 June 1966

Mary and I hitchhike to Newcastle for my sister Helen's wedding. She looks pretty in her pink suit and little green hat, and Mike is suitably handsome beside her. Her life appears to be going along the normal track, love, marriage, perhaps children. But, even though I am two years older than her, my life like Mary's is unsettled, wild, uncertain. We have boyfriends but neither of us has met our true love, the one we could adore for the rest of our lives. My mother feels that Helen is settled but worries about me. She knows that I have a plan to travel the world.

Injections
Hereford, 5 July 1966

Once back in Hereford, my friends are preparing for new jobs while I have injections against unknown diseases in foreign lands. Poland, yes, but I also have an idea to go as far as Israel, and who knows where afterwards. I'm immunised against smallpox, typhoid, cholera, yellow fever, polio and diphtheria. My dentist ensures that I have a healthy mouthful of teeth, and I complete my first aid kit with codeine and anti-malarial tablets.

And Mary and I learn that, despite our inattentiveness and poor attendance at lectures, our boredom with Dutch ports and isobars, we have managed to achieve a C average for our geography course. We've scraped through.

The Dance
Hereford, 8 July 1966

This is the last real day in college. The end-of-year formal dance is tonight. Boys are arriving from Ireland and London and Birmingham. Gar had arrived last night and he had slept in the bushes by the front lawn. We girls give our presents to the kind cleaners who had put up with us over the years, and we sang "For They Are Jolly Good Fellows" to them, with our musical accompaniment. My diary:

> *All afternoon we were madly finishing our dresses, sewing, talking, boys kept arriving, the Irish lads in ones and twos, the London lads in a group. They all went off boozing while we girls were getting on each other's nerves, looking for stockings, white petticoats, roses. Then someone wanted their hair doing, sewing was hastily going on, and then finally I discovered as I completed my dress that it was useless. So I threw it in the bin and began a search for another.*
>
> *Eventually, the lads having scrambled into their suits, we were all ready and off we went to the dance. Nobody ever realised before that we could look so smart, all the girls lovely*

in their dresses and the boys so handsome in their suits. Ralph, Gerry, Geoff, Leo and Gar, from London, Scotty the American boy from Birmingham, Garnet from Hereford, Gar, Len, Jem, Kevin, Gene from Dublin. On our side, Jenny, Mary, Jean, Janet, Becky and me. Tonie was happy with her Ivor. The best part of the dance, which was wonderful, was when we all danced in a circle. Even our favourite men lecturers with their wives joined us.

After the dance, we all circled away in the moonlight, and it was a matter of finding a place for them all to sleep. As it was the last night of term, we smuggled them into our hostel. Some stayed in my room and Jenny's. Others, me included, slept on the balcony. It was relaxing lying outside, just like being on holiday, and I felt in harmony with life despite the fact that it rained in the night and we had to creep back inside.

Leaving
Hay-on-Wye, 9 July 1966

We are breathing deeply, looking at each other, packing our last-minute belongings in bags. One by one the girls in our hostel are leaving. Some are taking taxis to the railway station, others carrying their bags to the bus station. A few, certainly not the majority, have parents who turn up in cars. All our disjointed, sleepy, untidy friends are tumbling onto the lawn, overlooked by the college's tall brick towers.

We'll go to Hay. We decide to meet by the river, at the Warren. In dribs and drabs, we make our way along the familiar A438 road out of Hereford. My diary:

Everybody loves being by the riverside. I do especially because of so many memories of the past and they are all like a set of scenic photographs in brilliant colours in my mind. It's the brown earthy banks, the fields of green corn and grass, the hills tree-covered behind, and the sharp blue and cloudy sky. It's the sound of silent moving water, echoing birdsong, grass whispering a little, waving buttercups. It's the warm earthy smell of soil and grass, all bursting fertile life.

Everyone was there, all happy to be together. At times, we all feel the unity and love between everyone in the group, and no-one knows where it comes from, or why it is. But it is there. It comes and it goes, a person fades then joins again but everyone sticks together marvellously on the whole.

I am having comforting conversations with Gene from Dublin. He is a small boy, shorter than me, with a crop of red hair and a fine interesting face. His eyes are so blue that sometimes they appear not to be looking at anything. He was likely to burst into a cheeky teasing laugh at any time, and he always sang.

I am thinking that soon I shall be leaving these parts for a long long while, and that probably this is the last time I'd ever hitch the

South Wales roads from Hereford. Strange how it is possible to love a place, to feel a sense of knowing and belonging, to feel that this indescribably beautiful part of the country belongs to me, and I to it. It is a joy to share the lovely views and tiny places in woods and fields with people like these. They love it too. I feel that only bad luck or change of fortune will prevent me coming back this way.

Len from Dublin is dressed in a top hat and a black duffle coat and is close to beautiful Jenny, with her long legs and brown wavy hair. While we are at the Warren, Scott and I sit on the diving board, he playing his banjo and me, barefoot, my tin whistle. The music is as important as ever.

My diary:

> That evening, we all went to the Black Lion and we practically filled the pub with people. My sister Helen and her new husband Mike suddenly turned up, on their way back from their honeymoon in Tenby. At the pub closing time, it was difficult because no-one knew where to go. In the end some went to the empty station to sleep, and others including me took our backpacks and slept under Hay bridge.

There we build a fire, pass around cigarettes and drink a little more before tumbling into woodsmoke-scented dreams.

On The Black Mountain
Hay-on-Wye, 10 July 1966

There is a place that draws us. This is the mountain that faces over the borders of Wales, the one I had looked at so often from my blue room in the student hostel, its strong, distant form overlooking the Wye valley.

There is a narrow road that leaves Hay, heading upwards

towards the mountain. We follow it, some on foot, others in Garnet's car. My diary:

> We suddenly realised that, at long last, after three crammed-full years, we'd finished college. The impact of this knowledge which we'd calmly accepted until then suddenly hit us, but we didn't have scenes of tears or sorrow. We became aware of an immediate, challenging future, the old ties leaving us to shoot forth as pellets from a catapult. We felt the strength of our independence, the force of our natures to carry us clean living and free into a new life.
>
> A merry gang assembled at the signpost by New Forest Farm, and there was dancing and joking and foxgloves appearing in the car.

I take a photograph of all of us, clustered around and on top of Garnet's car. A barefoot Jenny is with Len in the front, and Geoff is next to them, rolling a cigarette. Gerry and Ralph, whom Mary and I had first met in Tunisia, are behind. Mary, wearing flip-flops, is crouching with Gene. Leo is waving from behind, with Jean, Garnet, Scott and one or two others in the rear. I am not in it because I had taken the photograph.

It starts to rain. We must go a little higher. It is as though we must establish our existence, our release, in the presence of the mountain. The road narrows and steepens, climbing past ancient coppiced-hazel trees growing out of stony banks beside the road. This is the boundary of the enclosed farmland and the pastures of the hills, and we ascend to the open area where the white sheep are grazing. My diary:

> *We went up onto the mountain, the wind beating rain at our faces and buffeting all around us. Mary, Jenny and I danced together, wildly and necessarily, not needing to hide our feelings because the boys as usual tolerated everything. I felt my soul carefree and flying freely as I was only a body being contorted and soaked by the elements. The rain seeped in until I was soaked, hot blood raced around me and kept me warm, exhilarated, considering only a wild desire for freedom. It was freedom of our individual souls which wanted to burst free and exhale their strength and power, cleaned by wind and rain.*

Change

Returning to the others, we spend that night camping by a hedgerow in the mountains, cooking our food on a wood fire, and shaking ourselves down into the new people we must become.

11

Scattering

Hereford, July 1966

There is a silence now, for a day or two, at Hereford College of Education. We have left. The boys who were attracted into our centre will have no reason now to hitchhike along the roads from Dublin, London, Cornwall. Soon, other girls will take our places. My little blue room with its view over towards the sunsets of Wales will have a new occupant.

Down in the cathedral, the *Mappa Mundi* will rest quietly in its gloomy aisle for the time being, quiescent, silent, trapping into itself the places and journeys of the long-distant past. The roads arriving in Hereford that we'd learned to negotiate from our sixpenny road maps are now leading us away. It has been *sweet and fair to walk for the country,* here on the borders of Wales, and widely over the lands through which we've travelled. We are scattering outward, in all directions, into new untravelled worlds of womanhood, towards adventure, love, perhaps sorrow too.

Eastward
Towards Berlin, 1 August 1966

With my pack on my back, I am walking towards the border crossing at Helmstedt–Marienborn between West and Communist East Germany, heading for Berlin. Jenny and I had parted in Cologne two days ago after travelling together for a fortnight through France and Switzerland. I'd waved her off on a lift that would take her all the way to Aachen.

Most of the few cars on the autobahn have B for Berlin on their numberplates. The road feels less welcoming than any of those I have hitchhiked along during the past three years. As I walk between lifts, policemen on motorcycles go roaring by, a single girl on foot and heading east being of little concern. I am approaching the militarised Soviet zone of Germany, which I must cross on my way to Poland.

Mary is hitchhiking through the forests of Finland. Tonie is secure with Ivor in Wales. Jenny is probably already back home and will soon reimmerse herself into the network of our friends.

I am feeling the sorrow of separation. My friends will start their new jobs as teachers. Perhaps I will return to that one day. Now I am alone. I am struggling between the world I have left behind and the desire for adventure that draws me on.

I shiver a little as the road leads me eastward.

12

Epilogue

My book *Cold War, Warm Hearts* tells what happened after I separated from Jenny in summer 1966. I travelled in the countries behind and beside the Iron Curtain for over a year. Along the way, I met Bill, a young American man whose beguiling smile, good looks and courtesy won my heart. We fled from Germany when he was called up to do a second two-year stint in the US army, this being the time of the Vietnam War. After marrying, we lived in the USA and then Northumberland, where we still live. We brought up four children and now have six grandsons. He became a beekeeper like my father. I worked in the environmental movement, finally becoming a proper teacher in my fifties as an English tutor with people from overseas.

After we finished college in summer 1966, the links between the friends I'd left behind evolved, and new relationships formed. Some worked out, and some did not.

Jenny taught in Birmingham for a couple of years before moving back to the home counties. She married Geoff and they had three sons. After being left to rear her boys alone, she updated her qualifications and became a teacher in Berkshire. She has six grandchildren. She says that the three years in Hereford were among the best in her life.

Mary completed her probationary year teaching in Birmingham, during which time she met and fell in love with Damien from Dublin. They hitchhiked to Israel in 1967, stopping to work in Germany along the way. They married in England in 1969 and then moved to Ireland, where they still live. They have three grown children and nine grandchildren. Mary studies ecology and botany, and swims wild in the sea.

Tonie was a successful teacher for thirty-five years, finishing up as deputy head of a primary school in Pembroke Dock. She married Ivor, and they had one son. She kept on with folk music, playing the melodeon in the Vagrants Crew, with her later long-time partner Phil. She has lived all her life in Wales and lives close to her three grandchildren.

Chris enjoyed dance at college, but the boys in the tough London school where she taught didn't appreciate it. She had a long and varied teaching career culminating in several years helping children with special needs. Her youth hostelling days evolved into tackling long-distance footpaths.

The long-suffering Miss Eleanor Hipwell oversaw great changes after we left. From 1966, the college began to accept men and mature students. In 1975 the government closed sixty-nine colleges throughout the country, including Hereford, from which time university degrees were required for teachers. The building became the Royal National College for the Blind in 1978, and then in 2013 the degree-level campus for Hereford College of Arts, which it remains at the time of writing. Miss Hipwell, unknown to us at the time, was a highly respected member of INSEA, the International Society for Education through Art, and became its president in 1969. She travelled worldwide, and after her retirement acted as a magistrate in Hereford. It seems a shame now that we didn't appreciate her. We could have had interesting interactions if it hadn't been for the huge gulf between remote authority and the rebellious students of those days. She died in 1995.

Further Reading

General

Sarah Arrowsmith, *Mappa Mundi, Hereford's Curious Map*, Logaston Press, 2015.

As students, we knew of the *Mappa Mundi* in Hereford Cathedral, and had visited it. Its significance at the centre of our lives in the city became important to me as I wrote these stories.

Jack Kerouac, *On the Road*, 1957, and *Big Sur*, 1966, various publishers. At the time of my stories, in the 1960s, I knew these books. The influence of the "travellin' man" was strong in the folk music circles.

Spain

Laurie Lee, *As I Walked Out One Midsummer Morning*, first published 1969.

The author left home aged nineteen in 1934 and walked into Spain at the time when the Civil War was building up. Captures village life and poverty and the drama of Spain. Despite the Civil War and World War II intervening, Spain didn't seem much different during our visits in the Franco era of the 1960s. Highly recommended.

Laurie Lee, *A Moment of War*, first published 1991.

Tells of his short time as a volunteer in the international brigade during the Spanish Civil War. Superb writing describing the hopelessness, bravery, suffering, pointlessness of it all.

Laurie Lee, *A Rose for Winter*, first published 1955. My version Penguin 1971.

In 1949, he revisits Spain and some places he'd travelled to in 1934. The Civil War has left its relics in Spain under Franco. He laments the poverty, writes lyrically about the singing, the people, the dramatic Spain before being taken over by tourism. He describes the cruelty and drama of the bullfight. Highly recommended.

Antonio Cazorla Sánchez, *Fear and Progress: Ordinary Lives in Franco's Spain 1939-1975*, Wiley Blackwell, 2010.

This book reveals the harshness of life for the ordinary, the poor, people of Spain. It describes famine until 1959, hunger and hardship after that, and people who had learned not to speak out about politics. It exposes emigration, lack of sanitation, severe shortage of housing and no significant health service, aspects of which my friends and I only saw superficially.

Richard Wright, *Pagan Spain*, Harper Collins, 1957.

This brilliant book was written just a few years before our three visits. If we'd known all this before going to Spain it would have influenced all we saw.

It includes details of the sneering aristocrat who looks down on the powerless, the corruption of the church, the bullfight, Franco's regime based on naked force and the role of the Civil Guards with their black machine guns, the Spanish male's attitude to sex, the good women and the rest who were placed on earth by God to be exploited, white slavery, girls who line up to go to whorehouses in North Africa as a career opportunity, the pagan aspect of the processions in Spain's Catholic culture, and more. Highly recommended, even though much of this should now be history.

North Africa

Fatima Mernissi, *The Harem Within*, Doubleday, 1991.

Compassionate, intimate stories of life in her family's harem in Fez in the 1940s, with beautiful photographs by Ruth Ward. Pages 34 to 35 describe the harem as an extended patriarchal family rather like the one Mary and I had visited at Les Attafs in Algeria.

Albert Camus, *The Plague*, 1947, *The Outsider*, 1942, and *Summer in Algiers*, 1950. All available in Penguin.

I read them to get the feel of life during French rule in Algeria. The country gained independence in 1962, three years before Mary and I travelled there.

Douglas Porch, *Conquest of the Sahara*, Farrar, Straus and Giroux, 1984 and 2005.

Has excellent chapters about the reality of life in the Sahara as distinct from my romantic imaginings.

Guides to Tunisia, Algeria and Morocco

The *Rough Guides* to Tunisia and Morocco are always useful sources of cultural and historical information. A blitz of guides to Algeria has appeared since 2019, but finding anything around the time Mary and I were there in 1965 was difficult. The Berlitz Country Guide to Algeria, 1990, states: "You'll see plenty of hitchhikers… Some drivers will expect you to contribute to their costs. In the desert, the long, hot delays make it less enjoyable. Women, even in pairs or accompanied by men, should not hitchhike in Algeria. It simply would not be understood."

BOOKS I MENTIONED READING IN MY DIARIES
BETWEEN OCTOBER 1965 AND JUNE 1966

Oscar Wilde, *Picture of Dorian Gray*, October 1965

Alan Paton, *Debbie Go Home*, October 1965

Albert Camus, *The Fall*, October 1965

Mary Webb, *Precious Bane*, January 1966

Graham Greene, *Burnt Out Case*, January 1966

Walt Whitman, *Leaves of Grass*, February 1966

D H Lawrence, *The Trespassers*, March 1966

Jack Kerouac, *Big Sur*, March 1966

Maria Augusta Trapp, *Trapp Family Singers*, May 1966

Doris Lessing, *The Grass Is Singing*, May 1966

Margaret Mead, *Coming of Age in Samoa*, June 1966

Acknowledgements

Max Adams, Barbara Fox, Ian Leech; reading and commenting

Alison Hutchison; reading and fundamental guidance

Diane Milburn; reading and multi-lingual checks

Stephen Ashton; reading and critical guidance

Biddy Carrdus; meticulous proofreading

Colin Pearson; reading and IT

Mary Harris; original notebooks, stories and laughter

Jenny Head; stories and smiles

Tonie Jones; songs and poetry

Chris Vowles; stories and memories

About the Author

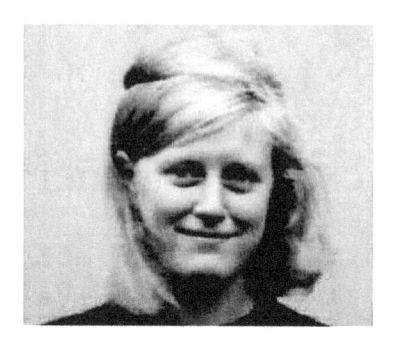

Bridget was born in 1944 and grew up in the Welsh border town of Hay-on-Wye. Her beekeeper father migrated with the family to Northumberland in 1955. From 1963 to 1966, she attended Hereford College of Education. Leaving college, she travelled alone, on foot, behind the Iron Curtain, writing extensive diaries and newspaper articles.

Back in Northumberland, she and her American husband raised four children and campaigned against nuclear power stations. During her varied working life, she has been press officer for Northumberland's anti-nuclear campaign, director of a renewable energy company, primary school teacher and lastly college tutor to overseas students learning English. After 1989, she travelled and photographed extensively in the countries she had visited in 1966 and 1967.

After writing a series of local history books about Northumberland, in 2022 she wrote a memoir about her childhood in Hay-on-Wye in the Welsh Borders: *Hay Before the Bookshops or The Beeman's Family*. This was followed by *Cold War, Warm Hearts*, 2023, and her new book, *Hit the Road, Gals*. These three stand-alone books have become *The Hay Girl Trilogy*.

Hit the Road, Gals is the third of Bridget Ashton's memoirs.

It follows ***Hay Before the Bookshops or The Beeman's Family***

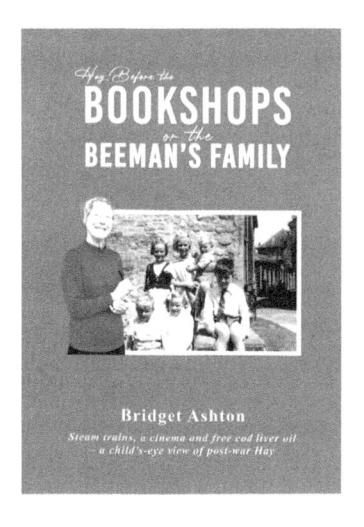

What they have said

"From steam trains to picnics in the castle, Bridget's new book, *Hay Before the Bookshops or The Beeman's Family*, has echoes of Kilvert's Diary as it lovingly recalls family life in post war Hay-on-Wye."

Joe Corrick, Journalist,
Brecon and Radnor Express

"This account of a post-war childhood was my holiday reading - and as compulsive as any page-turning thriller! Bridget captures beautifully the now-vanished world she grew up in, to create a book that is both a memoir and a fascinating piece of social history. The diaries of her poetic mother add another intriguing dimension to the tale."

Barbara Fox, author of
Bedpans & Bobby Socks and *When the War Is Over*

"A thoughtful memoir of one woman's childhood, with insights she has gained from her mother's life and personality, the family's rising and falling fortunes. With a father bent on an unlikely career as a beekeeper, things were not easy at home."

Alan Wilkinson, author of
The Red House on the Niobrara

"The times and the place both come to life vividly."

Mary Steele, editor of
Kilvert Society Journal

"If you want to know about life among ordinary British families at the end of King George VI's reign and start of Elizabeth II's, then read this book. Steam trains, ration books, strict schools, the new NHS. It's all there."

Ian Leech, journalist, editor of
Inside Morpeth

"The book presents a childhood memory of 1950s Hay-on-Wye before it became the bustling home of bookshops we so fondly know today. Its snapshot of Hay uses hand-written accounts from her mother's diaries."

Carrianne Lloyd-Ralph, journalist,
Wye Local

Letting the nine-year-old Bridget speak for herself guilelessly is the book's secret weapon! What a different world it was; and what an interesting family through which to encapsulate it.

Colin Pearson, academic and reviewer

and also published by The Book Guild, *Cold War, Warm Hearts.*

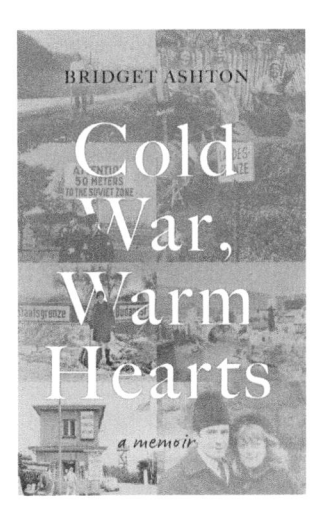

What they have said

"The warmth of your reception did not surprise me, nor the events, activities and people. What hit me 'out of the blue', so to speak, is the crystal clear, utter honesty of your prose, which arches over the events and physical happenings and reach deeply into the reader's soul, dragging back events, memories, places, colours, smells, loves, beauty, kindness and ugliness."

Henry Gulyas, Refugee from Hungary 1956

"Books based on diaries can become uneventful chronology, but not this one. The author's reactions to the kindness of strangers, the grim absurdities of the Soviet system and the biting cold are vivid. Reading it made me feel that I was there, sharing the experiences - a rare skill."
Lord Alan Beith, MP for Berwick upon Tweed 1973 to 2015

"What an amazing tale of discovery and adventure. I still cannot believe that a young woman travelled alone and on foot through the old Eastern Bloc countries in the late 1960s. Your meticulous diary entries describing your itinerary and the interesting people you met and the mishaps with your flip flops was a joy to read."
Frank Rescigno, Arts and Culture Director, Greater Morpeth Development Trust

"I must admit I was frightened for you at times! In many situations but particularly when you got so very cold when sleeping in a tent in the forest and later when you had men approaching your tent. The border guards seem to have been quite friendly considering their job. Still it was very unnerving to travel back and forwards over the Iron Curtain and very sad for people who were split from family and lands."
Dinah Iredale, author of *Bondagers* and *The Forgotten Workers*